THE
BIG BRITISH RAILWAY
PUZZLE BOOK

THE

BIG BRITISH RAILWAY PUZZLE BOOK

Journey your way through Britain with over 100
brainteasers, conundrums and train-related tests

National Railway Museum
with Roy & Sue Preston

SEVEN
DIALS

First published in Great Britain in 2020 by Seven Dials
an imprint of The Orion Publishing Group Ltd
Carmelite House, 50 Victoria Embankment
London EC4Y 0DZ

An Hachette UK Company

1 3 5 7 9 10 8 6 4 2

A CIP catalogue record for this book is
available from the British Library.

ISBN (Trade paperback) 978 1 4091 9756 0

Designed by us-now.com
Printed and bound in Great Britain by Clays Ltd, Elcograf S.p.A.

FSC
www.fsc.org

www.orionbooks.co.uk

CONTENTS

Section One

THE ORIGINS OF BRITAIN'S RAILWAYS

BRITAIN'S RAILWAYS BEFORE 1830

We can often take railways for granted. While they seem like such a simple technology, they have developed over centuries and the railway concept itself has humble beginnings. It is thought to have emerged from central European mining technology, which was brought to England by central European miners employed by the Society of Mines Royal during the 16th century. The society held a monopoly over gold, silver and copper mining in England and Wales, and mining railways were established at the Society's mines in Cumbria.[1] The type of railway adopted is known as the 'Hund' system and it reduced rolling resistance – a form of friction – making it easier to move heavy loads. Wide wooden rails guided Hund trucks carrying ore and spoil to the surface, these small, wheeled containers being moved manually by the miners themselves. Though primitive, this innovation incorporated the fundamental principles of a railway – it provided a track to guide vehicles over difficult terrain – and is a convincing beginning to the history of railways despite the precise relationship between the Hund system and subsequent developments remaining obscure.[2]

It was in the following century that developments in railway technology really picked up pace. In 1604, an English coal-mining entrepreneur, Huntingdon Beaumont, constructed a horse-drawn guided track above ground – known as a 'waggonway' – to link his colliery at Strelley, Nottinghamshire with the River Trent to overcome the disadvantage of roads rendered impassable by heavy traffic, particularly in bad weather. Beaumont's waggonway concept was subsequently taken to Northumberland, where he had obtained coal-mining rights from local landowners. This marked the origin of the vast networks of waggonways that would eventually spring up around the valley of the River Tyne.[3] By the mid-18th century, rail-based transport operated at several locations for different industries, ranging from the ironworks at Coalbrookdale to Middleton Colliery near Leeds.

The Railway Innovators

The late 18th century witnessed the spread of canal construction and so horse-drawn wooden waggonways and 'plateways' – a development of the waggonway that used cast-iron angled plates instead of wooden rails – were built to provide a cheap way of transporting goods traffic to canals in hilly terrain. In particular one plateway, the Merthyr Tramroad, which linked several ironworks to the Glamorgan Canal in South Wales, played host to the trial of a new form of technology – the Cornish engineer Richard Trevithick's steam locomotive of 1804. This was the first steam locomotive to haul a load on rails. Aside from hosting Trevithick's pioneering locomotive, South Wales was also the location of the horse-drawn Oystermouth Railway, which became the earliest paying passenger-carrying railway in the world on 25 March 1807.[4]

The following year, Trevithick trialled a new locomotive, *Catch Me Who Can*, in London. It was the first steam locomotive to haul fare-paying passengers, with one shilling charged for a ride on a temporary railway.[5] Problems with rail breakages under the weight of locomotives, however, hindered widespread interest in steam for the short term, while there were doubts about whether steam locomotives had the adhesion needed to haul heavy loads without additional engineering. In 1812, the coal-carrying Middleton Railway near Leeds was the first railway to successfully operate steam traction on a regular basis after John Blenkinsop developed modifications for both the locomotive and track. Teeth cast into the rails were designed to mesh with a powered gear wheel added to steam locomotives built by Matthew Murray, creating a 'rack and pinion' system that overcame the adhesion problem. In contrast, George Stephenson, an engineer working at Killingwoth Colliery on Tyneside, demonstrated that loads could be moved by a steam locomotive with smooth, self-guiding wheels running along the edge of smooth-topped rails during trials of his new locomotive, *Blücher*, in July 1814.[6] This concept is known as adhesion-working, in which a locomotive uses the friction between smooth driving wheels and smooth rails to gain traction and move a train.

Consequently, *Blücher* marked a further step on the road to the modern railway locomotive.

Turning Railway Visions into Reality

Despite the challenges of adopting steam traction, some individuals saw the potential for a national railway network long before its widespread emergence. Both Thomas Gray of Leeds and William James, a surveyor and land agent from Henley-in-Arden, had envisaged towns and cities being connected by a steam-driven railway system to improve the flow of people and trade.[7] However, such visions and ambitions awaited the emergence of malleable, wrought-iron rails capable of supporting a steam locomotive without breakage.

The first railway to adopt these rails was the Stockton and Darlington Railway, which was granted Parliamentary authorisation for construction in 1821. This railway was initially planned to be a horse-drawn waggonway using angled cast-iron plates. However, George Stephenson was approached by the line's principal promoter, Edward Pease of Darlington, to undertake a new survey of the proposed line to check and improve its route through the landscape.[8] On Stephenson's recommendation, it was decided to pursue steam traction and a new Act of Parliament authorised the various changes proposed. To obtain the required steam locomotives, Pease, Michael Longridge of Bedlington Ironworks, George Stephenson and his son, Robert, founded Robert Stephenson and Company in Newcastle, which built the railway's first locomotive in 1825. *Locomotion No. 1* was designed and built with the assistance of Timothy Hackworth, an engineer with previous locomotive-building experience, and would haul the first steam-hauled passenger train to run on a public railway from Shildon on the railway's opening day, 27 September 1825.[9] The Stockton and Darlington Railway thus marked the beginning of a transition from horse-drawn plateway to a modern railway system.

The First Modern Railway

It was the Liverpool and Manchester Railway, however, that drew together all the key components of the modern railway.[10] A line between the two cities had already been considered by Thomas Gray and William James, but it was not until 1821 that moves were made to build the railway, spurred by trader dissatisfaction with the performance of the Bridgewater Canal. Rates were high and progress slow on the congested canal, and a chance meeting between William James and Joseph Sandars, a Liverpool corn merchant, sowed the seed for what would become the world's first double-track inter-city railway operated with steam locomotives.[11] The use of double track helped increase line capacity as each line was given a specific direction of travel, allowing trains to run past each other without the need for passing loops, setting a template for future main lines to follow.

The team surveying the course of the line, successively led by William James, George Stephenson and the brothers John and George Rennie, faced opposition from the canal proprietors and local landowners, who sometimes resorted to violence. Consequently, it was not until 1826 that the necessary legislation was passed, and George Stephenson was reappointed as engineer, assisted by Joseph Locke. Construction included the creation of an embankment over Chat Moss – an impassable peat bog west of Eccles – the construction of a viaduct over the valley of the Sankey Brook and the driving of a railway cutting through Olive Mount at the Liverpool end. While the line was being finished, thoughts turned towards how it would operate; reliability problems with the locomotives on the Stockton and Darlington Railway, as well as a persistent belief among some engineers that adhesion-worked locomotives would struggle to haul heavy loads over long distances, meant that the use of steam traction was not inevitable. In 1829, the railway's management announced a competition to establish the suitability of steam locomotion: the Rainhill Trials. Five locomotives were tested over a short stretch of line to simulate everyday operation, although only one locomotive successfully completed the trials. This was *Rocket*, a locomotive entered by George Stephenson's son, Robert, which combined several features including a multi-tubular boiler and cylinders set at an angle from the vertical for the first time. *Rocket* had set the basic template for the steam locomotive.

On 15 September 1830, the Liverpool and Manchester Railway was officially opened with great pomp and ceremony in the presence of the Prime Minister, the Duke of Wellington. Eight trains were run in a procession from Liverpool Crown Street station, each conveying invited guests and paying passengers seeking to participate in the proceedings.[12] The lineside was packed with spectators; however, amid the sound and spectacle, a water stop at Parkside turned into tragedy. Although passengers were requested to remain in their carriages, several lowered themselves onto the track, and one, William Huskisson, a Member of Parliament for Liverpool who had championed the railway's cause in Parliament, sought an audience with the Duke of Wellington to bury political differences. With *Rocket* approaching, Huskisson panicked, grasping the door of the Duke's carriage before falling directly in front of the locomotive, which ran over his leg.

As a mortally wounded Huskisson was transported by rail with all haste to a vicar in Eccles, the reputation of rail transport hung in the balance – the Duke of Wellington was reportedly keen to abandon the run as a result of the accident.[13] After about an hour of discussion, fears of civil unrest being sparked by radicals demanding Parliamentary reform among the vast crowds assembled in Manchester meant a recommencement of the journey.[14] Although widely reported, the tragedy did not dent public interest in the venture and so, having survived this reputational setback, the Liverpool and Manchester Railway prepared the way for a national railway network. The events of September 1830 would spark a series of railway projects that would eventually see diverse regions of Britain connected to an extent unimaginable when Trevithick's locomotive made its first tentative moves on the Merthyr Tramroad 26 years earlier.

1. INDUSTRIALISATION WORD SEARCH

The early years of railways were all about labour, hard work and industry. The years of comfort and leisure travel were some way off prior to 1830. Find the listed words linked to industrialisation in the letter grid. They are all in straight lines and can go across, backwards, up, down or diagonally. There is one word that appears twice. Which is it?

ASSEMBLE	PIPES
AXE	PORTS
CARGO	PUMPS
COAL	QUARRIES
COLLIERY	RAIL
CONSTRUCTION	ROCKS
CONTAINERS	ROPE
FOUNDRY	ROUTE
FREIGHT	SEAM
IRON	SHOVEL
LIMESTONE	SLATE
LINE	TIMBER
LOAD	TOLL
MATERIALS	TONS
MILE	TRANSPORT
MINERAL	WAYS
MINING	WEIGHT
OPERATORS	WORKSHOP
PICK	

```
C O N S T R U C T I O N O L M
O G R A C N E N O T S E M I L
N U X O T O D A W A Y S O R T
T H G I E R F P O R T S L O O
A S H N H I A E R I T E N U L
I H I S B G R N K N V S C T L
N L I R O N T M S O E K L E Q
E D A O L I I L H P I C K U L
R A H T L N A S O D O O A A X
S R S A E I V E P L R R O R W
E A L R R M X U L A R C T E E
S I A E O A M I T I M B E R I
E L T P I P E S E G Z I K C G
A A E O S R A S S E M B L E H
M A M R Y R D N U O F D S E T
```

2. WHAT AM I?

My first is in **SLOW**
But isn't in **LOST**.

My second is in **CASE**
But isn't in **COST**.

My third is in **GATE**
But isn't in **LATE**.

My fourth is in **TOUR**
But isn't in **RATE**.

My fifth is in **TRAIN**
But isn't in **TRAM**.

Use all the clues
And say what I am.

3. ON TRIAL

It's hard to imagine the excitement that was generated by the Rainhill Trials when they took place.

The trials comprised 10 return trips along the 1.5 miles of track. The most successful engine, *Rocket*, managed an average speed of 12 miles per hour. It also managed to run at top speed at 30 miles per hour.

Put aside any time for restocking coal or water, and the fact that an engine has to build up steam to gain speed. If it had been possible to complete the trials running at full speed throughout, what would have been the difference in time between completing the trials at the average speed?

4. **WAGGONWAY**

As waggonways were not considered to be permanent routes, some landowners would not object to them – providing they didn't prove to be too troublesome.

Requests for four different waggonways have been made to run across this piece of agricultural land.

The owner is happy to give permission on the following terms:

• The waggonways must be completely straight.
• Each parcel of land is left with a barn, a lake and two areas of woodland.

Where were the waggonways situated?

5. A to Z

This puzzle looks like an ordinary crossword. However, there are no clues. The letters A to Z are each represented by a number instead. We have given you the numbers that represent the letters in the word **PIONEER** to start you off. All the answers in the crossword grid have a railway link. Most answers are made up of a single word, but also look out for two words that are often coupled together!

The checklist below will help you to keep track of the letters you have found.

I = **P**, 2 = **I**, 3 = **O**, 4 = **N**, 5 = **E**, 6 = **R**,

7 = , 8 = , 9 = , 10 = , 11 = , 12 = , 13 = , 14 = , 15 = , 16 = ,
17 = , 18 = , 19 = , 20 = , 21 = , 22 = , 23 = , 24 = , 25 = , 26 =

When you have filled in the crossword and worked out all the letters, look at the numbers below and find the name of a famous railway **PIONEER** from the early part of the 19th century.

6 2 13 26 10 6 8

7 6 5 14 2 7 26 2 13 11

1	2	3	4	5	6	7	8	9	10	11	12	13	14	15
	16		1		16				23		7		6	
6	10	14	2	4	5		24	9	10	6	6	2	5	25
	20		3		2				1		10		23	
1	21	10	4		22	10	7	5	25		8	3	3	6
	5		5		26		6				2		7	
6	10	13	5	8		1	10	25	25	5	4	22	5	6
	14		6		17			4	21		22			
	5			4	3	4	25	7	3	1			5	
			25		21		1		16		15		18	
8	2	6	5	13	7	2	3	4		7	6	2	1	25
	4		13					6	25		2		21	
12	21	10	7		23	5	7	10	21		7	3	3	11
	10		2		10				3		10		6	
9	4	21	3	10	8	5	8		1	6	2	19	5	25
	8		4		5				5		4		8	

6. CONNECTIONS

A vital part of a rail system is to have connections that allow you to change trains and move on to different routes.

In each case, find a railway word that connects the two given words. The answer must link to the end of the first word and go in front of the second word.

  1 DRIVING(_____)WRIGHT

    2 CAST(____)MONGER

      3 FULL(____)GAP

        4 COAL(____)FIELD

          5 STEAM(_____)DRIVER

7. MYSTERY OBJECT

Look at the **THREE** statements below and try to identify the mystery object.

If you get the answer after three clues award yourself a **SINGLE TICKET**.

If you get the answer after two clues award yourself a **RETURN TICKET**.

If you get the answer after one clue award yourself a **SEASON TICKET**!

I   The area around Durham and Newcastle dominated the production of this mystery object between 1700 and 1830.

2   George Stephenson's locomotive *Blücher* was designed to haul it on the Killingworth waggonway.

3   The proposed Stockton and Darlington Railway was originally intended to be used by horse-drawn wagons carrying it.

8. ROCKET WHEEL

The world-famous *Rocket* had twelve spokes on its large wheels. Answer the clues below and write the six-letter answers in the grid working from the outer edge of the wheel inwards. When you have finished, the first letter of each answer read in order will spell out the name of another locomotive from the early days of steam travel.

I   The name of a train, or Earth, Mars or Jupiter for example

2   Motor

3   George Stephenson's son

4   Tool for loading coal

5   Logo, symbol

6   It lies between hills

7   Enrols for a competition

8   The best speed to date

9   A climb up a hill

10 Opposite of wide, as in a gauge

II Bend

12 Use, give work to

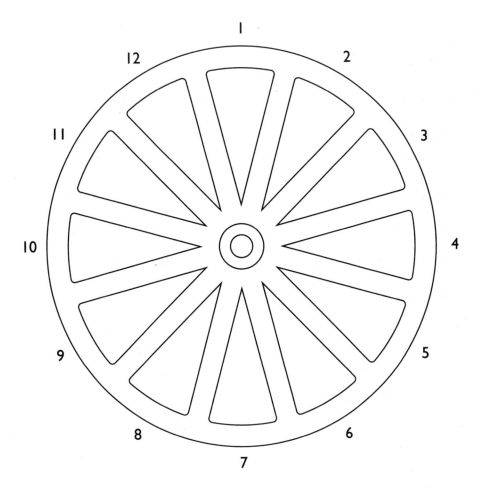

9. SINGLE TRACK

On a single-track railway, the down train and the up train share the same stretch of line.

This puzzle is just the same.

Answer the clues below, writing a single letter between each pair of sleepers, so that the letters work for both the down train clues and the up train clues. Down train answers read downwards and up train answers read upwards. The arrows next to the track indicate the starting point of each answer.

We have given you the number of letters in each answer with each clue.

When you have all the answers in place, take the letters in the shaded spaces and arrange them to spell out the name of a famous steam locomotive of the era. (Two words, 4 and 6 letters)

▼ DOWN TRAIN

Chief (**4**)

Cooking pot (**3**)

Travel by boat (**4**)

Chopping tools (**4**)

Part of a flower (**5**)

Wood or coal burners (**5**)

UP TRAIN ▲

Stroke of a letter (**5**)

Circuit of a race track (**3**)

County of South-east England (**5**)

Alternative name (**5**)

Dozes (**4**)

Weep (**3**)

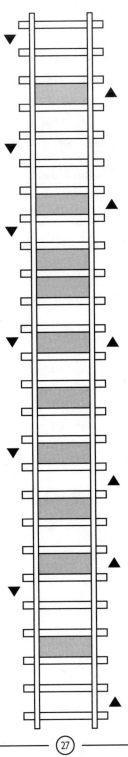

UP TRAIN ▲

10. QUOTA

Solve the clues and put your answers in the correct squares in the grid. All answers have EIGHT letters. When the upper grid is complete the first column reading down will reveal the name of a famous duke of this era. Transfer the key-coded letters to the lower grid and complete a quotation by him, which explains why he disapproved of railways. It begins, 'because they…'

1 Signalling instruments that you blow through.

2 Person who maintains locomotives.

3 Manual worker, responsible for the digging of land when railways were built.

4 Illumination, inside the train or on the track.

5 Originator of a design or machine.

6 Familiar or humorous title. Our mystery duke was often referred to as the Iron Duke.

7 The slope of a railway that rises from a horizontal level.

8 The final stopping place of a rail line.

9 Individual or company in charge of a railway business.

10 The early railways were largely in this area of England.

A	B	C	D	E	F	G	H
1							
2							
3							
4							
5							
6							
7							
8							
9							
10							

G1	B2	C6	G9	E3	H3	C7	C4	B8	■		
D10	D4	F2	■	A3	G5	A1	H6	B7	■		
B10	D9	D7	G3	H5	H8	■	E1	D3	■		
F9	H2	B3	C5	F7	F1	■	F6	C3	A9	G8	E4

ii. **SHAPE UP**

In this puzzle, letters have been replaced by shapes. The code is constant for all the railway-linked words below.

The first group of shapes reveals the name of the winner of the Rainhill Trials. (Forgotten the name? The info appears in this section.)

What do the other groups stand for?

1 ✻ ✮ ✢ ☆ ✢ ✳

2 ✢ ✿ ✻ ✳

3 ✳ ✻ ✿ ✢ ☆ ✳

4 ✧ ✿ ✳ ✢ ✳

5 ✢ ✿ ✻ ✻ ☆ ✿ ✧ ✢ ✳

12. ON THE MOVE

Many heavy loads were moved by train. The name of a type of cargo is hidden in each sentence below. Unearth them by linking words or parts of words together.

1   Engine driver Arthur is late for his shift yet again.

2   Workers in Mexico always have a break in the hottest part of the day.

3   Their only difficulty was the steep ascent outside the town.

4   Albert was the last on every journey to leave the train.

5   These locomotives were the first in the country to reach such speeds.

13. GOODS YARD

Can you find a route through the goods yard between the arrows? You must avoid the loaded carts, which are shown as black circles.

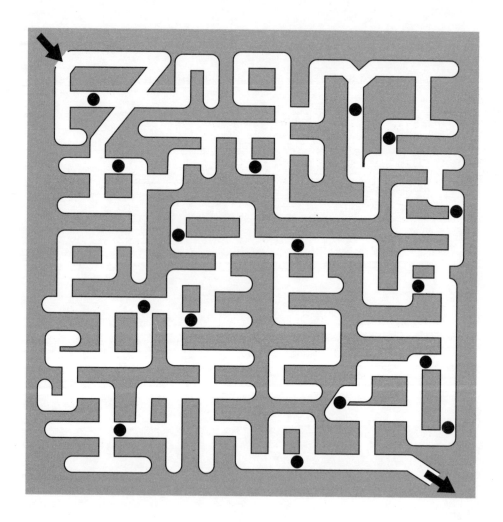

14. WHO IS IT?

Look at the three statements below. Consider yourself:

FIRST CLASS if you identify the mystery personality after the first statement.

SECOND CLASS if you are correct after the second.

THIRD CLASS if you need all three statements to reveal **WHO IS IT?**

1   His father, who was also an engineer, received no formal education but our mystery personality attended classes at Edinburgh University.

2   His first locomotive was called *Lancashire Witch*, and he shared a first name and an identical-sounding surname with a Scottish novelist and travel writer.

3   In 1829 he won the Rainhill Trials with *Rocket*.

15. PIONEERING PLACES

Famous names from the pioneering railway years have had their letters mixed up and rearranged in alphabetical order. Unscramble the letters, find the names and work out their location on the map of Britain.

I A D G I L N N O R T

2 E I L L O O P R V

3 A C E E H M N R S T

4 A H I I L L N R

5 C K N O O S T T

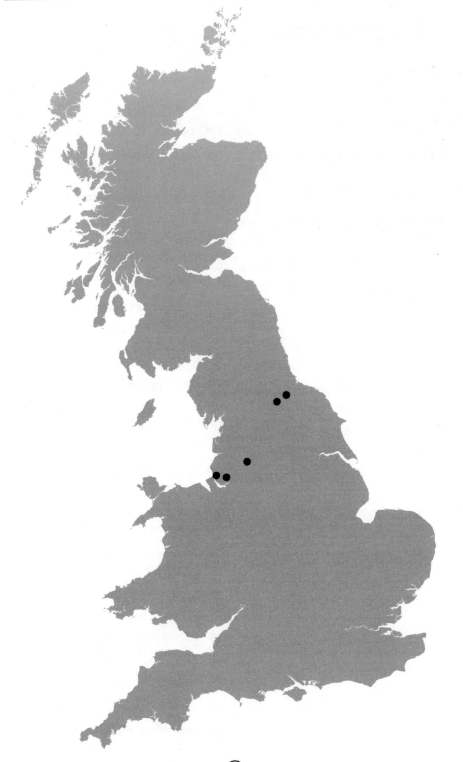

16. QUIZ TRAIN

All aboard to answer some quick-fire quiz clues!

ACROSS

3 It enables traction to the rail (5)

7 Isolated, railways made some places less so (6)

8 Be present at, as with the opening ceremony of the railway (6)

10 The lines, or courses in which trains move (10)

11 A short journey (4)

12 Grey rock, quarried in North Wales and transported by rail (5)

13 Which Timothy was working with Robert Stephenson in 1824? (9)

16 Open-topped carriers of heavy loads (7)

21 Which city was nearest to the site of the Rainhill Trials? (9)

22 White limestone in soil that had to be moved to create tracks (5)

23 Another word for a chimney (4)

24 Relaying messages via flags for example (10)

26 Control lever (6)

27 To introduce again, as some Heritage Railways did with old tracks (6)

28 Operate a locomotive (5)

DOWN

1 Conveyance for transporting people or goods (7)

2 Ericsson and Braithwaite's entry at the Rainhill Trials (7)

3 Was Darlington to the west or east of Stockton? (4)

4 Rules, regulations (4)

5 The first passenger one in the world was at 21 Across (7)

6 Which locomotive was built by Robert Stephenson, immediately after the *Rocket* in 1829? (7)

9 In 1827, 13 Across built this locomotive with a regal sounding name (5,6)

14 Whitstable harbour station was in which county? (4)

15 Vital piece of illumination equipment (4)

17 What was designer Hedley's first name? (7)

18 Those who have a special place in history are often so described (7)

19 Where was the first railway repair works? (7)

20 Made a strategy ahead of time (7)

24 Building to house a locomotive (4)

25 Unit of land measurement (4)

17. THE RAINHILL TRIALS

It is estimated that 10,000 people went to the Rainhill Trials in October 1829, such was the excitement surrounding the event.

The five individuals in this puzzle are part of that merry throng. Each gentleman is a member of a different profession, has a preference for a different locomotive and has made a guess as to how fast that locomotive will go. Use the information below so that you can fill in the upper grid. When you find a piece of positive information put a tick in the correct box. Put a cross when you have found a piece of negative information. Cross-refer until you can complete the box at the foot of the page.

1   Mr George's speed estimate was twice that of the estimate on *Perseverance*.

2   The farmer backed *Cycloped*. His prediction wasn't the highest speed.

3   Mr Charles, the miner, predicted the slowest speed.

4   If the speed prediction of the supporter of *Novelty* was added to the speed prediction of the seaman, the total would be the same as the prediction of Mr Ward.

5   Mr Andrews is not an engineer. His favourite was *Sans Pareil*.

		Profession					Locomotive					Speed Prediction				
		Engineer	Farmer	Grocer	Miner	Seaman	Cycloped	Novelty	Perseverance	Rocket	Sans Pareil	5 mph	10 mph	15 mph	18 mph	20 mph
Name	Mr Andrews															
	Mr Charles															
	Mr George															
	Mr Henry															
	Mr Ward															
Speed Prediction	5 mph															
	10 mph															
	15 mph															
	18 mph															
	20 mph															
Locomotive	Cycloped															
	Novelty															
	Perseverance															
	Rocket															
	Sans Pareil															

Name	Profession	Locomotive	Speed Prediction

18. SIDINGS

The sketch shows a length of track and sidings. There is an engine and a couple of wagons, numbered **1** and **2**.

There are three sidings – **A**, **B** and **C**.

B has the shortest length of track and only has space to take one wagon or the engine. It cannot house the engine when coupled to a wagon.

The wagons can only be moved with the help of the engine.

The challenge is for wagons **1** and **2** to swap positions, and the engine to return to its starting point, facing in the same direction. The engine's first move is not to reverse to siding **A**.

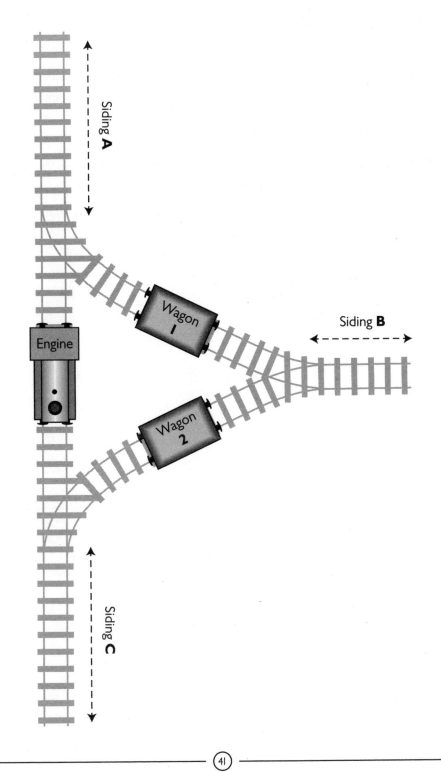

19. WHEEL-WRITE

Each wheel contains six individual letters. Two letters are shared with the other wheels. One question mark sign, which indicates a letter common to all three words, appears in the centre. Decide on the mystery letter, then use the letters to make three railway-linked words containing **NINE** letters each.

Set the wheels in motion and write the words below.

1 _ _ _ _ _ _ _ _

2 _ _ _ _ _ _ _ _

3 _ _ _ _ _ _ _ _

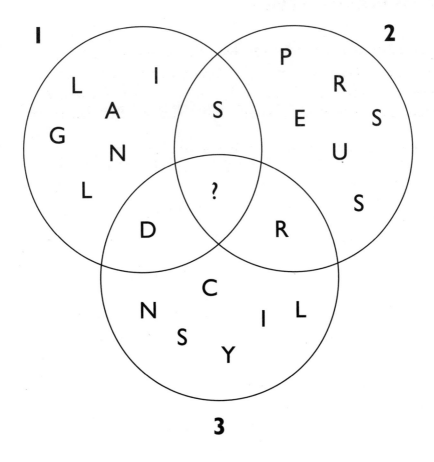

1

2

3

43

19. ROCKET ON

There is a reconstruction of the famous engine, *Rocket*, at the National Railway Museum in York.

Fit all the listed *Rocket*-related words back in place to read either across or down the grid.

There will be one word left over when the grid is completed. What is it?

3 Letters
PIN   ROD   SET

4 Letters
AXLE   BEND   BURN   COAL
HEAT   IRON   MILE   PIPE
RACE   SEAT   SHOW

5 Letters
CARTS   FLAGS   LEADS
LEVEL   LISTS   LOOPS
SHEDS   STEAM   TUBES
WATER

6 Letters
BOILER   BUFFER   ENGINE
PRIZES   ROCKET   SPEEDS
SPOKES   SPRING   WINNER

7 Letters
BALLAST   CHIMNEY
PISTONS

8 Letters
CONTROLS CYLINDER
RAINHILL SLEEPERS
SMOKEBOX

9 Letters
LIVERPOOL
METAL TYRE
NAMEPLATE

10 Letters
LOCOMOTIVE
MANCHESTER
STEPHENSON

13 Letters
DRIVING WHEELS

14 Letters
CARRYING WHEELS

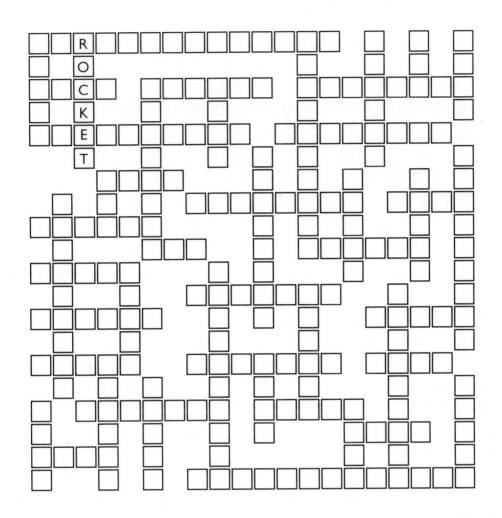

21. SPLITS

Carriages often split from the main train at various junctions en route.

In each of the groups below, two words of equal length with a railway link are split into two, although the letters are in the correct order chronologically.

What are the words?

1 CIORAONL

2 SWATEGAONM

3 ROWORUTKSE

4 GATURAGCEK

5 SWHMEOELKE

22. MEMORY TEST

——— **URGENT NOTICE** ———

PLEASE DO NOT LOOK AT THE QUESTIONS
BELOW. GO TO THE COLOUR PLATE
ON PAGE 1. STUDY THE POSTER FOR 2
MINUTES, THEN RETURN AND ANSWER
THE QUESTIONS BELOW FROM MEMORY.

1   Which is the earliest date on the poster?

2   Which railway company features in the top right-hand corner?

3   What is the name of the locomotive in the picture?

4   Who is driving it?

5   How many men are there in the picture?

6   Is the locomotive facing left or right?

7   What type of hat is the man on the right of the picture wearing?

8   How many wheels can you see on the side of the locomotive facing you?

9   Who is wearing the lighter-coloured outfit, the man on the left or the man on the right?

10   Which two words precede the dates at the top of the poster?

Section Two

THE RISE OF THE VICTORIAN RAILWAY

BRITAIN'S RAILWAYS 1830–1901

When Queen Victoria ascended the throne in 1837, few could have foreseen the explosion in railway investment, network growth and advances in railway technology that followed. While the Liverpool and Manchester Railway was successful after opening in September 1830 – the first few months of operation was spent meeting an unprecedented demand for passenger transport – the overall growth of railway investment was initially gradual.[1] However, in 1833, two major projects were authorised by Parliament on their second attempts: the 82-mile Grand Junction and the 112-mile London and Birmingham Railways.[2] Collectively, these formed the first long-distance main line, or 'trunk', railway in the world and would eventually connect London to the Liverpool and Manchester Railway at Newton Junction near Warrington. The pace began to quicken in the following years with the emergence of the London and Southampton Railway (1834) and the Great Western Railway (1835). However, the success of a few railways did not mean that opposition would cease overnight, as Parliament blocked some plans while disputes with landowners shaped the character of the railway network. One example was the sharp curve built to avoid the grounds of Stapleford Park in Leicestershire, which followed violent clashes between canal workers and railway employees after Robert Sherard, the 6th Earl of Harborough, 8th Baron Sherard and a shareholder in the Oakham Canal, opposed the construction of a line across his estate in Leicestershire.[3]

Another dispute arose on the question of the distance between the track rails – the 'gauge'. The majority of railways designed by George and Robert Stephenson had a gauge of 4 feet 8½ inches, which reflected both engineers' origins in North-east England as it approximates the width between the rails of the Killingworth waggonway. Although other engineers followed suit, Isambard Kingdom Brunel instead pressed the case for a wider track gauge of 7 feet ¼ inch between rails, citing improvements in speed and greater passenger comfort.[4] Brunel's 'broad gauge' was used on the new Great Western Railway (GWR) linking London and Bristol, blocking the creation of a truly national railway network, as symbolised by the fact that the company built its terminus at Paddington, rather than share the London and Birmingham's station at Euston.[5] The inconvenience of goods and passengers having to change from one network to the other meant Parliament stepped in to resolve the issue, settling on 4 feet 8½ inches as the new 'standard gauge' in 1846.[6] Although the Great Western was allowed to continue operating its existing broad-gauge network, it would eventually convert to standard gauge in 1892.

Railway Mania

Despite these disagreements, overall the pace of public investment gradually increased with investors purchasing company shares to make money from railway profits. A combination of the steady returns of railways such as the Stockton and Darlington and the Liverpool and Manchester, the ready availability of money from banks and the savings of aspirational individuals seeking to invest for the future and the desire of local business and political interests to link their towns to the trunk lines had prompted higher levels of railway investment in the 1840s.[7] The middle of the decade therefore witnessed the 'Railway Mania', a short period of intense investment and financial speculation in a rash of railway projects. Unchecked competition between companies could lead to bankruptcy and so the best way forward was amalgamation – the merging of smaller companies to improve financial stability. In this way, the 'Railway King', George Hudson, a York-based draper who inherited money and became a director of several railway companies, formed the Midland Railway in 1844.[8] Other amalgamations followed, including the London and North Western (1846) and the Manchester, Sheffield and Lincolnshire Railway (1847). Although the 'Mania' ended in a financial slump in 1847, the railway network had reached 6,600 miles of track by 1850; indeed, a subsequent 'Mania' occurred between 1861 and 1866, and the network comprised approximately 15,500 miles by 1870.[9] Railways had even been built in extremely mountainous areas, with engineers adopting a range of 'narrow' gauges to reduce construction costs and give access to quarries and mineral wealth – indeed, the Ffestiniog

Railway in Snowdonia had been in operation since 1836.[10] As for Hudson, who controlled over 1,000 miles of Britain's railway network, he was exposed as a fraudster in 1849, having misappropriated the finances of several railway companies.[11]

The Navvies

The construction of the railway network didn't just lead to financial gains for investors. It also absorbed vast numbers of labourers – the navvies. Many thousands were employed by railway contractors to construct cuttings, embankments and tunnels, initially with few mechanical aids. In 1838, the Great Western Railway's 2-mile Sonning Cutting alone employed 1,200 men and 200 horses on site.[12] Navvies were a mixture of skilled workers, itinerant labourers or members of the local population seeking short-term employment.[13] The latter included farm labourers in agricultural districts, although they deserted the railways during summer months for the hay harvest.[14] At the time, navvies were perceived as hard-living and hard-drinking social outcasts and became a constant in 19th-century Britain, moulding the landscape to meet the vision and ambition of railway companies and their investors. This, however, came at a cost in human lives – navvies lived in temporary settlements, sometimes in bleak and isolated terrain such as the Pennines, where there was a risk of disease. Conditions during tunnel construction were notoriously poor – at its peak, construction of the first Woodhead Tunnel employed 1,500 navvies and 32 lives had been lost by the time it opened in 1845.[15]

Much of the work of navvies is still standing today and bridges spanning navigable waterways are perhaps the most spectacular monuments to their ability to turn a civil engineer's design into reality. These range from Stephenson's Britannia Bridge (1850, severely damaged in 1970 and rebuilt in a different form in 1972) across the Menai Strait in North Wales; Brunel's Royal Albert Bridge (1859) across the River Tamar to Cornwall and the steel Forth Bridge carrying a railway across Scotland's Firth of Forth (1890), arguably the ultimate expression of Victorian civil engineering in Britain. There were disasters, however. Thomas Bouch's Tay Bridge spanning the Firth of Tay near Dundee collapsed just as a train was crossing the bridge in high winds on 28 December 1879, killing 75 people. Other iconic structures are viaducts spanning river valleys, with notable examples being Robert Stephenson's 28-arch Royal Border Bridge at Berwick (1850) and the Midland Railway's 24-arch viaduct at Batty Moss, Ribblehead (1875). The longest on the network is the 82-arch brick Welland Viaduct at Harringworth (1880).

Connecting the Country

The railway industry's position as a monopoly holder of long-distance passenger travel meant it began a close association with the Royal Family while it also played a role in facilitating social change, such as speeding up the mail and making leisure travel a mass phenomenon, rather than an activity of just the wealthy. With the network connecting urban sprawls to rural idylls, seaside resorts and golf links, railways became a means to explore the country on a scale hitherto unknown. Excursions could be organised by an agent, who negotiated cheap travel by selling tickets equal to the capacity of a railway carriage or an entire train and trips included visits to major national events, such as the Great Exhibition of 1851, educational visits, factory outings, attending religious meetings and even illegal prize fights.[16]

Along with other modes of transport, the railways were also a factor in shaping the social make-up of suburbs. As an example, Parliamentary authorisation for a railway extension to Liverpool Street in 1864 included a clause for running two early morning and corresponding evening trains at 2d as compensation for workers displaced as a result of construction.[17] This led to the creation of 'working-class suburbs' on the Great Eastern Railway's route, while the well-off left the city centre for rural suburbs in the south-west of London.[18] Despite benefiting the urban population, the railways were not always willing participants in transporting certain categories of passengers. Transporting the workforce at cheap rates was controversial as it meant providing facilities that found gainful employment for only part of the working day. However, Parliament was not deterred and another attempt to encourage the railways to run more third-class trains found fruition through the Cheap Trains Act of 1883, which offered tax relief on journeys charged at under 1d per mile.

Although passenger travel had, almost unexpectedly, established itself as the principal revenue-earner for Britain's railway industry by the mid-19th century, 1852 was the year in which freight became the main source of income, a situation that was to last for over a century.[19] Freight was broadly split between minerals and 'merchandise', a category encompassing anything from manufactured goods to perishables. The expanding network saved time and reduced the penalty of distance, enabling the marketing of agricultural products throughout the country instead of at their place of origin, where prices might otherwise have been lowered by too much supply and not enough demand. Speed was also important for high-bulk, low-value commodities such as coal and minerals, which experienced widespread demand that outgrew the capacity of canals to maintain a reliable supply. The railways therefore permitted an increase in scale for industrial enterprises and, in doing so, they became highly sensitive to shifts in the wider economy.

Improvements in Rail Safety

With traffic growth, safety became a rising concern. Basic measures such as semaphore signalling, the electric telegraph, 'block' working and interlocking were developed to regulate trains on specific sections of track. Block working entailed the division of routes into fixed sections, blocks, that were controlled by signals and their signallers to maintain safe distances between trains, while interlocking provided a mechanical link between the points guiding trains from one line to another and their corresponding signals to prevent collisions caused by signaller error.

However, investment in new safety technology was at the discretion of the railway company. Companies frequently viewed safety devices as a costly extravagance that risked reducing staff competency, while their adoption was not mandatory.[20] Accidents inevitably stemmed from dangerous working practices, oversights or penny-pinching.

As an example, the Sonning accident on the Great Western Railway on Christmas Eve in 1841 highlighted the third-class passenger's plight, as the company routinely coupled its open-topped third-class passenger carriages between the locomotive and goods wagons. On this particular day, a train ran into a landslip caused by heavy rainfall and eight passengers were immediately killed when their carriage was crushed by the following goods wagons.[21] The inquest recommended that carriages should offer greater protection to this class of passenger and should be attached to the rear of mixed trains.

The conditions in which third-class passengers travelled became a focus of the Railway Regulation Act of 1844. This helped to establish a minimum standard of passenger accommodation by making fully enclosed carriages a statutory requirement.[22] Although grudgingly implemented by the railway companies, the comfort of all classes of passenger eventually became an important selling point. This change in approach was triggered by the Midland Railway, which introduced comfortable third-class passenger accommodation on all its services from 1872.[23] Two years later, the same company imported the first luxury Pullman carriages from America, beginning a series of developments in passenger travel that included on-train dining on the Great Northern Railway from 1879 and electric lighting on the London, Brighton and South Coast Railway from 1882.[24] However, a lack of enforcement in other areas of railway safety and operation meant that it wasn't until the late 1880s that real change would occur.[25]

The accident that made the adoption of basic safety measures compulsory through an Act of Parliament took place at Armagh in 1889. An overloaded school excursion train was divided on a gradient to allow a portion to be hauled over the summit. Although the train had a vacuum brake, it was not automatic, and the rear portion had to be secured using rocks; this proved ineffective, and the carriages rolled back down the gradient before colliding with a following train, killing 80 passengers including 22 children.[26] The Regulation of Railways Act was passed two months later, which required all railways to adopt fail-safe automatic brakes on passenger trains, implement block working and adopt signal interlocking. By the end of the century, the railways had come of age as movers of freight and passengers at high speeds underpinned by basic safety standards, becoming the only way to travel for millions of people.

1. BOOKSTALL

In 1848 W.H. Smith opened the first station bookstall at Euston station.

Look at the clues below and work out the identity of an author whose works would have been widely read during this period, and also the name of one of his many novels. It was one of the first to feature this new mode of transport.

1   The novel was written the same year the first railway bookstall was opened.

2   The author initially despised the railways as he could see how they destroyed the countryside. He was himself a victim of a railway accident in 1865.

3   The book describes the impact of the railways; he called the London and Birmingham Railway a 'great earthquake'. The 'Son' in the book's title was called Paul.

2. STATIONGRAM

Rearrange the letters to spell out the name of a station.

CRY HOT LIP

3. QUOTA

Solve the clues and put your answers in the correct squares in the grid. All answers have **EIGHT** letters. When the upper grid is complete the first column reading down will reveal the name of a character from *The Importance of Being Earnest* by Oscar Wilde. Transfer the key-coded letters to the lower grid and complete a quotation by that character, who reveals a location where something significant was unfortunately mislaid in the book.

1 Sacks for holding large numbers of letters.

2 Gentle slopes for railways often in the countryside.

3 Places where trains stop so passengers can join or leave the train.

4 Describes people or places north of the border.

5 Raised paved area parallel to the track when the train stops.

6 This word describes a seat that has been booked and cannot be used by anyone else.

7 First name of pioneer Brunel.

8 Causing a train to be diverted down a siding.

9 John Tawell, apprehended via GWR's telegraph system in 1845, was this type of criminal.

	A	B	C	D	E	F	G	H
1								
2								
3								
4								
5								
6								
7								
8								
9								

F6	E2	C2	E8	F3	E6	C1	C7		D5	B8	E9	
E1	H9	A7	H8	H4	D3	F5	F2		B5	F4	G3	G9

4. SINGLE TRACK

On a single-track railway, the down train and the up train share the same stretch of line.

This puzzle is just the same.

Answer the clues below, writing a single letter between each pair of sleepers, so that the letters work for both the down train clues and the up train clues. Down train answers read downwards and the up train answers read upwards. The arrows next to the track indicate the starting point of each answer.

We have given you the number of letters in each answer with each clue.

When you have all the answers in place, take the letters in the shaded spaces and arrange them to spell out the name of a destination that was more accessible after the building of the Forth Railway Bridge in 1890.

▼ DOWN TRAIN
Set fire to (**4**)

Era (**3**)

Boast (**4**)

Second hand (**4**)

Subsequently (**5**)

Liberated (**5**)

UP TRAIN ▲
Antelope (**4**)

Show distress (**4**)

Diminish (**4**)

Sweetener (**5**)

Started (**5**)

Press firmly over a surface (**3**)

▼ **DOWN TRAIN**

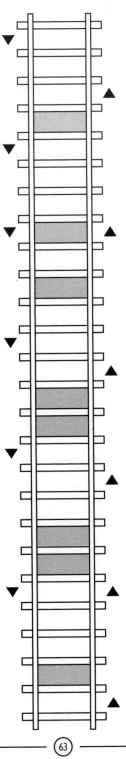

UP TRAIN ▲

5. TURNTABLES

Turntables enabled a train engine to be physically moved around. It meant that at the end of a line the engine could swing half-circle and then be facing the direction it was about to travel.

In March 2020 excavation work for the High Speed 2 railway uncovered a turntable designed by Robert Stephenson at Curzon Street, Birmingham, which opened in 1838.

Here's a sketch of a vast goods yard full of lots of turntables. An engine can only change direction when the turntable moves. The engine can only move on and off a turntable when the tracks connect. Turntables can make quarter, half or three-quarter turns. You can make a complete whole turn – but then you would be heading back the way you came!

Find a route so that an engine can move along the tracks from arrow **A** to arrow **B**.

How many turntables have to turn?

In which direction – north, south, east or west – are most changes made?

Our Centenary This London and North Eastern Railway poster uses artwork by Fred Taylor to commemorate the centenary of the opening of the Stockton and Darlington Railway in 1925.

Catch Me Who Can by Richard Trevithick was demonstrated to the public near Euston Square in 1808, and the scene is captured in this watercolour by Thomas Rowlandson, although the year was incorrectly cited as 1809.

Locomotion No 1 Terence Cuneo's 1949 oil painting, *The Opening of the Stockton and Darlington Railway*, captures the spectacle of September 1825.

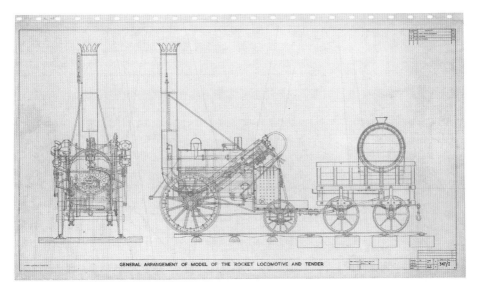

Locomotive Plan An engineering drawing of Robert Stephenson's *Rocket* (1829). It was drawn by Ernest Forward for a 1:8 scale model of the locomotive, c1908.

Liverpool Crown Street station *Railway Office, Liverpool* (1831), an aquatint by S. G. Hughes from a drawing by Thomas Talbot Bury. It depicts the Liverpool and Manchester Railway's original Liverpool terminus at Crown Street, which hosted the start of the railway's opening cavalcade in September 1830.

left

Isambard Kingdom Brunel Robert Howlett took this image of Isambard Kingdom Brunel during an attempted launch of his ship, the *Great Eastern,* in 1857. Brunel was appointed the Great Western Railway's chief engineer in 1833.

below

4-2-2 broad-gauge locomotive Tice F. Budden took this image of a 4-2-2 'Rover' class broad gauge locomotive hauling a Plymouth express at Ealing in 1890. Although a standard gauge of 4 feet 8½ inches between rails was set by Parliament in 1846, the Great Western Railway was allowed to continue operating its 7 feet ¼ inch broad gauge. The image shows dual-gauge track, which can be compared with the standard gauge lines to the left of the picture.

Over a Century of Progress (1933) uses artwork by E. H. Fairhurst to demonstrate the latest development of the steam locomotive on the West Coast route, the London, Midland and Scottish Railway's express passenger 'Princess Royal' Class.

George Hudson An engraving of the 'Railway King', George Hudson, by James Andrews, c1850. A citizen of York, Hudson would eventually control over 1,000 miles of Britain's growing railway network. He was eventually exposed for financial irregularities in his railway interests.

Navvies at Dove Holes Tunnel Navvies during the construction of Dove Holes Tunnel in Derbyshire. Completed for the Midland Railway in 1865, the tunnel was part of a new route to Manchester via Rowsley. Armed with picks, shovels and wheelbarrows, the dangerous working conditions endured by the navvies is evident.

Coal wagons at Ocean Colliery Coal was almost synonymous with the railways, which carried vast quantities. This is one of the Ocean Coal Company's South Wales collieries, c1885. Before Britain's railways were nationalised in 1948, the majority of coal wagons were privately owned by collieries, merchants and wagon builders.

Milk Freight Porters unloading milk churns at the Midland Railway's Somers Town goods depot, London, c1890. The railways were crucial in transporting perishable foods such as milk from the country to the city, ensuring steady supplies to meet the demands of the capital's growing population.

Pullman car Topaz The luxurious interior of Pullman car *Topaz*, built 1913. The Midland Railway imported Pullman carriages from the United States, and the first entered service in 1874. In contrast, the interior of everyday coaching stock was much more functional.

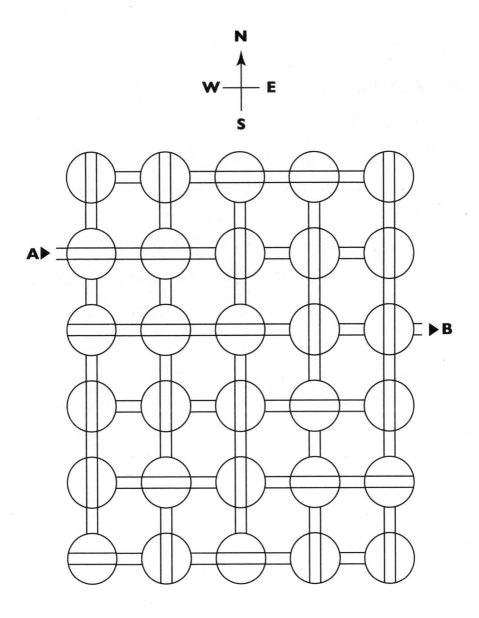

6. WHO IS IT?

Look at the three statements below. Consider yourself:

FIRST CLASS if you identify the mystery personality after the first statement.

SECOND CLASS if you are correct after the second.

THIRD CLASS if you need all three statements to reveal **WHO IS IT?**

1   His father Sir Marc designed a shield that allowed safe excavation of tunnels.

2   He was appointed engineer of GWR in 1833 at the age of 27.

3   He was instrumental in establishing a line between London and Bristol.

7. STATIONGRAM

Rearrange the letters to spell out the name of a station.

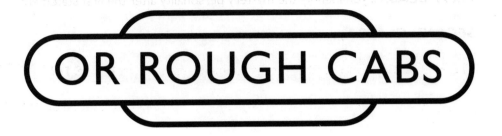

8. RAILWAY COMPANIES WORD SEARCH

Railway companies, large and small, sprang up during the Victorian era. Many amalgamated to form larger companies and some were short-lived due to financial problems. Find the names of railway companies below in the letter grid. They are all in straight lines and can go across, backwards, up, down or diagonally. Where linked names are on separate lines in the list, they are separate in the grid.

BARRY

CALEDONIAN

CAMBRIAN

CLEVELAND

EASTERN COUNTIES

FFESTINIOG

FURNESS

GRAND

  - JUNCTION

GREAT

  - WESTERN

HIGHLAND

ISLE OF MAN

MERSEY

METROPOLITAN

MIDLAND

NORTH

- LONDON

RHYMNEY

SNOWDON

- MOUNTAIN

SOUTH DEVON

SOUTHERN

TAFF

- VALE

E	A	S	T	E	R	N	C	O	U	N	T	I	E	S
M	L	R	N	Z	Q	Y	L	T	O	A	V	B	R	G
E	D	I	E	O	R	D	A	V	F	E	N	X	H	L
T	G	N	B	R	W	U	E	F	W	A	D	A	Y	Z
R	O	C	A	L	E	D	O	N	I	A	N	O	M	U
O	I	B	E	R	H	J	O	R	L	D	A	E	N	A
P	N	W	S	T	G	R	B	N	H	N	L	R	E	W
O	I	N	U	I	T	M	A	I	X	A	E	D	Y	E
L	T	O	A	H	A	M	G	A	V	L	V	C	S	S
I	S	D	P	C	F	H	U	T	S	D	E	L	S	T
T	E	N	G	O	L	J	A	N	A	I	L	T	E	E
A	F	O	E	A	X	A	O	U	L	M	C	A	N	R
N	F	L	N	J	A	R	S	O	U	T	H	E	R	N
E	S	D	Y	E	S	R	E	M	Z	E	N	R	U	R
I	J	U	N	C	T	I	O	N	P	P	C	G	F	N

9. FARE DEAL

In the early days of rail travel there was much discussion and deliberation about how much to charge the British public for using the fast-expanding rail network. Distance travelled? Quality of carriages? Number of routes available?

In this puzzle we drop in on a young, enterprising, London-based booking clerk who has come up with an innovative, but totally impractical method of price-fixing for travelling by train. Here is his suggested list of charges for destinations outside London. How has he worked out these fare deals?

Note – in pre-decimal days there were 12 pennies in a shilling, so any fare that cost more than 12 pennies is shown in shillings and pence (e.g. 25 pennies would be 2 shillings 1 pence or 2s 1d).

1 BRIGHTON – 7s 9d

2 GLASGOW – 7s

3 LEEDS – 3s 9d

4 PENZANCE – 7s

5 YORK – 5s 9d

10. FORWARD SHUNT

Solve the quick clues below. In this puzzle there is no shunt or diversion down a siding. However, you might be sidetracked as the answer to the second clue contains almost the same letters as the first, but in the second answer the middle letter has been shunted forward in the alphabet.

1 Railway line – Freight wagon

2 Carriage – Comfortable seat

3 Financial interest – Feed the furnace

4 Small disc as an award – Iron, tin, steel

5 Stairs – Ceases

11. **RECTANGULAR RAIL**

Railway companies of all shapes and sizes sprang up during this era. Here's a plan of 16 linked stations, on a network of straight-running track. The distance in miles around the biggest rectangle is 80 miles.

A rectangle is a shape with four straight sides and four right angles, each of 90 degrees.

Individual rectangles can be grouped with other rectangles to make new rectangles.

  1 How many rectangles appear in this plan?

  2 How many miles is the journey around all sides of the smallest rectangle?

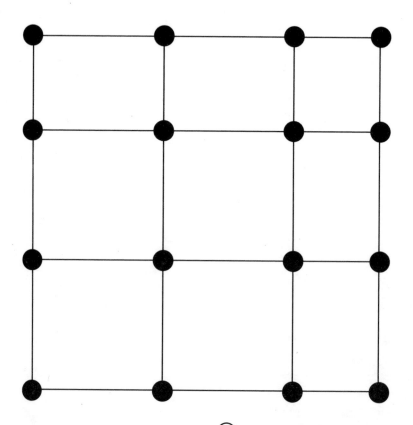

12. SPLITS

Carriages often split from the main train at various junctions en route.

In each of the groups below two words of equal length with a railway link are split into two, although the letters are in the correct order chronologically. What are the words?

1 BRGAUAKRDE

2 STRPEUCEKD

3 LITNRAEINS

4 BTRUNINDEGEL

5 PSIOINGNTSAL

13. A to Z

This puzzle looks like an ordinary crossword. However, there are no clues. The letters A to Z are each represented by a number instead. We have given you the numbers that represent the letters in the word **BRISTOL** to start you off. GWR completed the important link from London to Bristol in 1841.

The checklist below will help you to keep track of the letters you have found.

1 = **B**, 2 = **R**, 3 = **I**, 4 = **S**, 5 = **T**, 6 = **O** , 7 = **L**,

8 = , 9 = , 10 = , 11 = , 12 = , 13 = , 14 = , 15 = , 16 = , 17 = , 18 = , 19 = , 20 = , 21 = , 22 = , 23 = , 24 = , 25 = , 26 =

When you have filled in the crossword and worked out all the letters, look at the numbers below and find the name of the oldest station in this West Country city.

5 26 17 23 7 26

17 26 9 25 4

14. FITBACK – ENGINES

Here's a list of engine names. Some are well known and some less well known.

Fit all the listed words back in place to read either across or down in the grid opposite.

There will be one word left over when the grid is completed. What is it?

3 Letters

TAY

4 Letters

ASIA   BUTE   IONA
IRON   DUKE   SPEY

5 Letters

ARRAN   HEROD
MADGE

6 Letters

AFRICA   EGBERT
EUROPA   PLUTUS
TARTAR

7 Letters

ACTAEON   AMERICA
ARDROSS   DERWENT
EADBALD   HENGIST
VOLCANO

9 Letters

GLADSTONE
JENNY LIND
NORTH STAR

10 Letters

STEPHENSON

11 Letters

DUNALASTAIR

12 Letters

SHOEBURYNESS

13 Letters

LADY OF THE LAKE

16 Letters

GORDON HIGHLANDER
WHITE HORSE OF KENT

15. **CONNECTIONS**

A vital part of a rail system is to have connections that allow you to change trains and move on to different routes.

In each case, find a railway word that connects the two given words. The answer must link to the end of the first word and go in front of the second word.

1 SCOTCH(_____)TRAIN

2 HAND(____)WAY

3 MAIN(____)DRAWING

4 SINGLE(_____)SUIT

5 RAILWAY(_____)CLOCK

16. SPECIAL SCOTCH EXPRESS

In 1862, the *Special Scotch Express* was introduced. It was nicknamed the *Flying Scotsman* because of its extraordinary speed. Its journey took it from Kings Cross in London to Edinburgh Waverley station and from Edinburgh Waverley back to London.

The journey time for the distance of around 400 miles was 10 hours, including a meal break that took place in York and lasted 30 minutes.

On this particular day the *Special Scotch Express* left Kings Cross as usual at 10 a.m. It was travelling at an average speed of around 40 miles per hour. Each train had 10 carriages. The northern-bound train was fully booked, whereas the one heading south held only half its capacity.

Unfortunately the train leaving Edinburgh was delayed by 30 minutes and did not leave Waverley station until 10.30 a.m. Its average speed was 34 miles per hour.

By the time the trains passed each other, which train was nearer to Edinburgh Waverley station?

17. LOST PROPERTY

In recent years East Midlands trains revealed some of the more unusual items left behind by passengers. These included a selection of musical instruments, a prosthetic leg and a 7ft surfboard.

Going back to earlier train travel, the five rail passengers in our puzzle haven't lost anything quite so bizarre but they still needed to visit a lost property office as a precious item has been mislaid. Each traveller started their journey that day at a different time and arrived at a different London railway station. Use the information below so that you can fill in the upper grid. When you find a piece of positive information put a tick in the correct box. Put a cross when you have found a piece of negative information. Cross-refer until you can complete the box at the foot of the page.

1   Mr Guard started his journey half an hour after the lady who lost her spectacles. Neither arrived at Paddington station.

2   Mr Driver was not the person who started their journey at 8 a.m. and came into Liverpool Street.

3   The traveller who mislaid their raincoat arrived at Waterloo. They weren't the person who set off first or last on their day's journey.

4   Mr Porter had the earliest start heading for Euston station but fortunately did not lose his keys.

5   Miss Stokes left behind her umbrella.

	Item Lost					Station					Time Started				
Name	Keys	Raincoat	Spectacles	Umbrella	Wallet	Euston	Kings Cross	Liverpool St	Paddington	Waterloo	6.00 a.m.	6.30 a.m.	7.00 a.m.	8.00 a.m.	9.00 a.m.
Mr Guard															
Mr Driver															
Mr Porter															
Miss Stokes															
Mr Whistler															
Time Started															
6.00 a.m.															
6.30 a.m.															
7.00 a.m.															
8.00 a.m.															
9.00 a.m.															
Station															
Euston															
Kings Cross															
Liverpool St															
Paddington															
Waterloo															

Name	Item Lost	Station	Time Started

18. MYSTERY OBJECT

Look at the **THREE** statements below and try to identify the mystery object.

If you get the answer after three clues award yourself a **SINGLE TICKET**.

If you get the answer after two clues award yourself a **RETURN TICKET**.

If you get the answer after one clue award yourself a **SEASON TICKET**!

1 From 1882, side corridor carriages allowed passengers to access these during a journey.

2 Previously in 1869 the first purpose-built example was fitted in the Royal train.

3 Queen Victoria was the first monarch to find these a convenience on her journeys to Balmoral and the Isle of Wight.

19. FUEL FOR THOUGHT

Shovelling coal on a steam locomotive was not for the faint-hearted. In old weights and measures there were 112lbs in a hundredweight and 20 hundredweights in a ton.

If a locomotive needed 40lbs of coal to travel 1 mile, how many tons would it need to travel the number of miles that were the same number as the number of pounds in half a hundredweight?

20. GWR

The GWR is known as the Great Western Railway (also God's Wonderful Railway or the Great Way Round, depending on your views). There is no doubt that GWR opened up the west of England so that you could travel to London and back on the same day.

Famous names from the golden GWR years have had their letters mixed up below and rearranged in alphabetical order. Unscramble the letters, find the names and work out their location on the map of Britain.

I BILORST

2 EEERTX

3 AADDEEHIMN

4 ADEGINR

5 DINNOSW

21. GRADIENTS

With steam trains the pressure was well and truly on to move at speed. Different terrains presented different challenges. It's always harder going uphill than downhill!

• A train travels at an average of 60 miles per hour on level track.

• It travels at an average of 40 miles an hour when moving down a sloping gradient.

• It travels at an average of 30 miles an hour when having to climb up a gradient.

What is the difference in time between a train travelling from A to E and a train making the return journey from E to A?

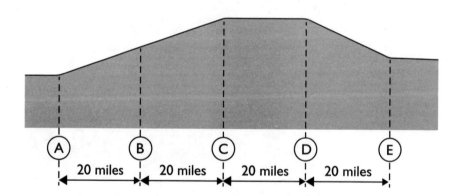

22. WHAT AM I?

My first is in **FIRST**
And also in **LAST**.

My second is in **FUTURE**
And also in **PAST**.

My third is in **TRAVEL**
But isn't in **TRACK**.

My fourth is in **FORWARD**
And also in **BACK**.

My fifth is in **MOVES**
And also in **SAME**.

Use all the clues
And give me a name.

23. QUIZ TRAIN

All aboard to answer some quick-fire quiz clues!

ACROSS

3 The Midland Railway Locomotive works was founded here (5)

7 Which Stephenson was considered to be the father of the railways? (6)

8 Was used for the first time, as with the Skegness Railway in 1873 (6)

10 What was the surname of Cornish inventor Richard, and son Francis? (10)

11 At the back (4)

12 A stand for selling newspapers (5)

13 Yorkshire city linked with a Manchester and Lincolnshire company (9)

16 E stands for this in NER (7)

21 This is the most northerly railway junction in Britain (9)

22 Lakes, accessible through railway expansion north of the border (5)

23 Norfolk station between Stowmarket and Norwich originally proposed by the Ipswich and Bury Railway (4)

24 London terminus for East Coast Main Line to Edinburgh Waverley (5,5)

26 Fame, notoriety (6)

27 Dock Street station was opened in this east coast Scottish city in 1857 (6)

28 Distance between a pair of rails (5)

DOWN

1 Which Cumbrian town linked with Cockermouth and Keswick in the name of a railway company that formed part of a route linking Workington and Durham? (7)

2 Makes journeys (7)

3 Amount owed, the problem of many early railways (4)

4 The *Special Scotch Express* stopped for a meal break in this city (4)

5 Nickname for someone from the North-east (7)

6 Comes off the tracks – unintentionally (7)

9 The Caledonian sleepers were these vehicles (5,6)

14 Payment for a trip (4)

15 Speed contest (4)

17 Wiltshire town whose station opened a week early in 1846 (7)

18 Brunel wanted to link London with this city (7)

19 Taking longer journeys for pleasure (7)

20 Which city links to Holyhead in the name of the company involved in the mail route to Ireland? (7)

24 George Hudson was known as the Railway what? (4)

25 Not the front or the back (4)

24. FOURTH BRIDGE

Spanning the Firth of Forth, construction on this famous landmark bridge started in 1882 and was opened in 1890. It shouldn't take as long as that to solve this puzzle, but it isn't straightforward! Beware of heading down a track which leads to a dead end!

All the railway-related words contain **FOUR** letters, and you have to fit them back to construct a bridge where all words link. Words can read across or down. One letter is in place to start you off.

AREA	PASS
CARS	RIDE
COAL	RUNS
DOOR	SEAT
EAST	SPED
EXIT	SPOT
LOAD	STOP
MAPS	TOUR
MOVE	UNIT
OPEN	USED

25. STATIONGRAM

Rearrange the letters to spell out the name of a station.

26. MEMORY TEST

────── **URGENT NOTICE** ──────

PLEASE DO NOT LOOK AT THE QUESTIONS
BELOW. GO TO THE COLOUR PLATE
ON PAGE 5. STUDY THE POSTER FOR 2
MINUTES, THEN RETURN AND ANSWER
THE QUESTIONS BELOW FROM MEMORY.

1 Which railway company's name is at the bottom of the poster?

2 What is the oldest locomotive named on the poster?

3 Which 'Royal' name is to the right of the picture?

4 Which way is the locomotive facing?

5 Which word follows, 'Over a Century of'?

6 Which is the earliest 19th-century date in the background?

7 How many windows in the cab are visible on the poster?

8 The sketches that form the background to the poster are of what?

9 How many locomotives are named on the poster altogether?

10 Other than black and white, what is the predominant colour here?

Section Three

RAILWAYS IN WAR & PEACE

THE RAILWAYS AT THEIR ZENITH
1901–1950

The first decades of the 20th century saw Britain's railways reach their zenith in mileage and scale. By 1913, route mileage had reached 20,088 miles and further construction was broadly restricted to creating new connections whenever and wherever new opportunities for business were identified. While the railways had changed the pace of urban development through the creation of new suburbs in the Victorian era, the process began to slow in the 1900s as the expense of building houses combined with a slowdown in wage growth to restrict demand for suburban housing to those with plenty of money.[1] It was apparent that residents needed the flexibility and finances to afford both the property and regular rail fares.[2]

Some companies looked to technology to reduce costs, with widespread main-line railway electrification under active consideration from 1902 – once installed, it was a cheaper alternative to steam traction as it required fewer staff to run and was more flexible than the steam locomotive in operation. Both the Lancashire and Yorkshire and North Eastern Railways commenced passenger and goods electrification schemes around Liverpool and Shildon respectively, while the London, Brighton and South Coast Railway considered converting its South London Line, which was partly justified as a response to the rising local competition from electric trams.[3] Indeed, the tram spurred the use of the steam rail motor, essentially a steam-powered passenger carriage, by the London and South Western and Great Western Railways, the latter heading off the threat of a tram route between Cheltenham, Stroud and the Golden Valley by providing a new service for local villages.[4]

Alongside the improvements in passenger travel, freight – ranging from cattle to milk and from steel to chocolate – was being carried by rail over long distances. In the case of cattle, the railways had already made long-distance droving redundant, allowing cattle to be sold on in better condition.[5] For milk, the railways were instrumental in the creation of

London's long-distance milk trade, with milk cooled in churns transported in ventilated vehicles from countryside to bustling metropolis in a matter of hours, while confectionery firms such as Rowntree's of York and Cadbury's of Bournville used a full range of railway services, including condensed milk and fruit transport and the storage and onward distribution of their chocolate products at goods depots around the country.[6] However, a global war was about to change the environment in which the railways operated.

The First World War and its Aftermath

The outbreak of the First World War in August 1914 saw the railways operated as a single entity by a Railway Executive Committee of key railway managers working on behalf of the government. Although they initially operated on a 'business as usual' basis, such an approach could not continue after 1915 as hopes of a quick war receded, coupled with rising train weights and greater demands made by military recruiters upon railway staff.[7] In 1915, women began to replace railwaymen called up for military service, being initially allocated to unskilled roles.[8] While opposition from male colleagues ensured this arrangement lasted only for the duration of the conflict, women were given roles with greater responsibility as the war progressed.[9] In a broader sense, the war also highlighted demands for better pay and conditions. With the railways a crucial industry, demands for better working conditions were met for the duration of the conflict.

After the war, the railway industry sought to reduce costs by lowering rates of pay, sparking the 1919 railway strike. While the strike was disruptive, an alternative form of transport was on the horizon – the motorised lorry. Lorries had been used on a small scale before the war, but were expensive to buy and maintain.[10] Thousands were built for military service during the war and were available to be pressed into emergency road operations. Consequently, the 1919 strike was an opportunity to see what the lorry could do, and their ability to maintain supply lines in an emergency had impressed businesses such as milk wholesalers and confectionery manufacturers. After the war, many surplus military lorries were purchased by ex-servicemen who subsequently entered the road haulage business, and their ability to provide a cheap and accountable door-to-door service signalled their potential as a competitor to rail transport.[11]

The effectiveness of the railways as a unified operation during the First World War prompted debate on how they should work in peacetime. The choice was outright nationalisation or a reorganisation into fewer private companies with regional monopolies but competing on long-distance routes. The Railways Act of 1921 took the latter course, and around 120 companies were grouped into four large firms: the Great Western; the London, Midland and Scottish; the London and North Eastern; and the Southern Railways. These were very different organisations to the companies that share the same names today. The legislation also called for a major revision of freight rates that ultimately failed to account for growing road competition, which continued to make inroads into railway traffic after the 1926 General Strike.[12] This, coupled with the onset of economic depression in 1929, began four difficult years for the railways. Income after expenses and other deductions had reduced from £45 million in 1929 to £29 million by 1932, which accompanied a 24 per cent fall in freight tonnage.[13]

The effects of the Depression were not the same for all of the railway companies. The Southern Railway was primarily a passenger-focused concern, and its general manager Herbert Walker championed the development of its suburban services through electrification to increase traffic and reduce operating costs. Furthermore, government development loans enabled the railways to continue investing in new infrastructure and equipment to provide employment opportunities.[14] The 1930s was also a period of adjusting to road competition, with campaigns to lobby government seeking to secure much more favourable financial terms. To this end, two major publicity campaigns were waged – *Fair Play for the Railways* in 1932 and the *Square Deal* of 1937, but neither had any lasting effect.[15] Financial hardship provided the backdrop to the mid-1930s, a period otherwise described as the 'golden age' of the railways, during which advertisements sold speed and comfort, and the epitome of British steam locomotive design was reached with the introduction of the London and North Eastern Railway's Class A4 (1935) and the London, Midland and Scottish Railway's 'Princess Coronation' Class (1937) streamlined locomotives.

An Essential Utility:
The Railways in the Second World War

The high-speed exploits of these locomotives made the headlines, although this flourish of public spectacle was ended by the outbreak of the Second World War. The risk of fuel shortage meant that the railways were the natural choice for moving troops, armaments and food supplies. The railways were also key in the evacuation of children and vulnerable adults from cities susceptible to air attack that took place from 1 September 1939, and were brought under government control two days later. A new Railway Executive Committee coordinated operations, while services and speeds were reduced to save scarce labour, materials and line capacity. In contrast to the First World War, many grades of railway worker were exempt from conscription and there was little hesitation in employing women in many customer-facing, operating and maintenance jobs, with the London, Midland and Scottish Railway alone employing 39,000 women across 250 job grades.[16]

Britain's railways were essential during the evacuation of the British Expeditionary Force and French troops from Dunkirk and elsewhere in northern France in May–June 1940, and railway-owned shipping was pressed into naval service. Several ships were lost as a result of enemy action at a high cost in lives; the London, Midland and Scottish Railway steamer TSS *Scotia* sank with the loss of around 300 crew and servicemen.[17] The railways were also key to dispersing troops upon arrival in Britain, with the line between Ashford and Redhill bearing the majority of the effort – 377 troop and ambulance trains composed of locomotives and rolling stock from several companies were squeezed through the latter junction over the course of the evacuation.[18] On the operating side, posters exhorted civilian passengers to travel only when necessary throughout the conflict, while railway workshop capacity was turned over to tank, gun and machine parts production. Consequently, 'Austerity' locomotives such as Oliver Bulleid's Q1 Class of 1942 were designed for quick and easy construction with the minimum of material resources.

Like the rest of the country and its industries, the railways also experienced aerial bombardment. During the night of 10 May 1941, 711 tons of bombs were dropped over central London in nearly five hours, causing significant damage to goods and passenger stations; however, debris was quickly cleared and damage repaired to ensure the trains kept moving.[19] The fighting spirit was also shown with railway personnel volunteering in Air Raid Precaution, fire and Home Guard roles, while railway headquarters were moved to rural areas surrounding London to ensure continuity of control in emergencies. Even with milk distribution, emergency road-rail transhipment points for pumping milk into road tanks were established on the outskirts of London to reduce delays caused by bomb damage or line congestion.[20] Up to a quarter of a million gallons of milk were transferred in this way in 1941 alone.[21] The railways continued to play a crucial role in the war effort, and supported the Allied invasion of Normandy in 1944.[22] All of this came at a price, as six years of constant use, minimal maintenance and war damage had taken their toll by the time the war ended in 1945.

Nationalising Britain's Railways

A newly elected Labour government sought to bring the railways into public ownership as part of its policy of nationalising the 'commanding heights' of British industry.[23] The government also nationalised long-distance road haulage, thereby intervening in road-rail competition by using public ownership to coordinate both. Nationalisation was bitterly opposed by the railway companies; it was considered a distraction that delayed their post-war investment plans.[24] The uncertainty surrounding the future of the railways and continued shortages of materials also meant delay in addressing the wartime maintenance backlog; consequently, the period 1945–1947 was characterised by further deterioration, prompting the Chancellor of the Exchequer, Hugh Dalton, to exclaim that the railway companies were 'a very poor bag of physical assets'.[25]

Despite railway companies' protestations, the Transport Act was passed in 1947, authorising the nationalisation of Britain's railways on 1 January 1948. The new structure was centred upon a new strategic planning authority, the British Transport Commission, which would oversee the operations of a series of Executives responsible for managing the day-to-day work of the various transport enterprises.[26] The Railway Executive comprised former railway managers who oversaw the process of change as the four railway companies were split into six geographical regions. The first two years of nationalisation were subsequently spent binding together the former companies into a single organisation, as symbolised by the question of establishing a standard identity and trialling the locomotives of the former companies on different routes, ostensibly to establish which features could be used in future designs.[27]

In 1950, the decision was made to pursue the construction of a new generation of steam locomotives, as coal was relatively cheap and in plentiful supply, while a continuing shortage of materials meant that electrification was restricted to only a few projects such as the Sheffield to Manchester route via the Woodhead Tunnels. The result was the development of 12 new 'standard' steam locomotive classes. However, this was done at the expense of developing diesel locomotives, of which only a few prototypes had been tested. This was partly due to the cost of importing oil, and partly because of the low initial cost of steam, although its continuation failed to account for post-war staffing shortages and rising wages. However, Britain's fragile post-war economy, in which food was rationed and steel was in short supply, meant that much-needed investment to refresh the tired railway network remained beyond reach.

1. MURDER ON THE MIDNIGHT EXPRESS

Brigadier Cuthbert Crusty has hosted dinner in his private compartment on the late-night express train from Paddington, the *Midnight Express*. Joining him for dinner were five guests, each of whom had a specific link to the great man. The purpose of the dinner was to discuss Lord Crusty's forthcoming biography, which promised to reveal some hitherto hidden secrets about his long life. At the end of the meal each guest goes their separate way on the train, leaving Lord Crusty alone except for his bottle of vintage port. On the stroke of midnight one of the waiters comes into the compartment to clear everything away, only to find Lord Crusty slumped at the table, the port glass in his hand. The waiter feels for a pulse but it is too late. Clearly the drink has been poisoned and one of the guests must have substituted a bottle of poisoned port for Cuthbert's original tipple. A fellow passenger on the train is Inspector Calls from Scotland Yard. All the rail staff are excellent witnesses and provide the following information. After they left Lord Crusty each of his guests was seen in a different part of the train. Each was carrying a different item. You can join Inspector Calls in finding out who committed the crime.

Look at the information below. When you find a piece of positive information put a tick in the grid. Put a cross when you find a piece of negative information. Cross-refer until you have completed the lower grid and then take a look at the inspector's notes. The murderer will then be revealed.

1. Professor Wilde, the ex-colleague, was seen in a 2nd-class carriage.

2. Claude Battersby-Smythe was not in the corridor, which is where the solicitor was seen, carrying a cane.

3. Myrtle Overbrightly was seen in a 1st-class carriage carrying a typewriter; Lord Crusty's cousin was seen carrying flowers.

4. Lord Tony Broke, who wasn't Lord Crusty's cousin nor his personal assistant, wasn't seen with a tray, but was seen in the sleeper.

Inspector Calls made a few notes. The 1st-class carriage was too far away from the scene of the crime to be of relevance. The guests seen with the tray and the briefcase could not have substituted the bottle. The briefcase was far too small, you would see a bottle on a tray! The solicitor was in the clear as keeping Lord Crusty as a client was to their advantage. So, who is the murderer?

		Link					Carrying					Location				
		Biographer	Cousin	Ex-colleague	PA	Solicitor	Briefcase	Cane	Flowers	Tray	Typewriter	1st Class	2nd Class	Corridor	Restaurant	Sleeper
Name	Claude															
	Tony																
	Myrtle																
	Olga																
	Prof. Wilde																
Location	1st Class																
	2nd Class																
	Corridor																
	Restaurant																
	Sleeper																
Carrying	Briefcase																
	Cane																
	Flowers																
	Tray																
	Typewriter																

Name	Link	Carrying	Location

2. STATIONGRAM

Rearrange the letters to spell out the name of a station.

NEVER SINS

3. FAMOUS NUMBER

One of the most famous locomotives of all time proudly displayed a four-digit identification number on the side of the cab.

If the third digit and fourth digit were multiplied together the answer would be the same number as if the second and third digits were taken out, and the first and last digits read together.

The first two digits are the same, and there are no odd numbers involved.

What is the number?

4. A to Z

This puzzle looks like an ordinary crossword. However, there are no clues. The letters A to Z are each represented by a number instead. We have given you the numbers that represent the letters in the word **EXPRESS** to start you off. Most answers are made up of a single word, but also look out for two words that are coupled together!

The checklist below will help you to keep track of the letters you have found.

1 = **E**, 2 = **X**, 3 = **P**, 4 = **R**, 5 = **S**,

6 = , 7 = , 8 = , 9 = , 10 = , 11 = , 12 = , 13 = , 14 = , 15 = , 16 = , 17 = , 18 = , 19 = , 20 = , 21 = , 22 = , 23 = , 24 = , 25 = , 26 =

When you have filled the crossword in and worked out all the letters, look at the numbers below and find the name of a famous **EXPRESS** train from this period.

18 6 4 6 10 13 22 19 6 10

5 18 6 22

	18		18		5			15		19		8		
26	13	12	6	24	22		5	22	13	10	23	13	4	23
	4		24		13			11		12		13		
19	4	6	10		4	19	23	15	1		7	19	10	25
	19		22		22		19				7		18	
18	13	4	4	12		6	21	1	4	10	19	15	14	22
	15		12		13		1		1		18			
	1			1	2	3	4	1	5	5			20	
			7		7		5		22		16		24	
18	13	9	1	22	1	4	19	13		22	24	4	10	5
	7		19				6		22		13		18	
5	19	22	5		3	1	10	18	1		7	13	22	1
	15		24		13				4		19		19	
18	14	13	4	15	19	10	15		17	6	22	19	6	10
	22		1		23				5		12		10	

5. A PENNY A MILE

In 1935, **LMS**, **GWR**, **LNER** and **SR** commissioned an advertising poster to publicise their journeys at a 'penny a mile'. This was for a return journey completed within a month, although first-class passengers paid a penny ha'penny for the same distance (i.e. half as much again per mile.)

Mr Tripp bought four tickets for his family so that they could all make a return journey taking advantage of this very special offer. As head of the family, he decreed he would travel first class. At the station he handed over a 10 shilling note for all the tickets, and received a shilling in change. How long was the Tripp family's return journey?

(**BEWARE**: These are pre-decimal days!)

6. CLOCKWORK

Find a route along the tracks so that there is never more than one hour's difference between the times shown on the station clocks on the journey. Start at the station clock on the far left horizontal middle line and finish at the right of the same line.

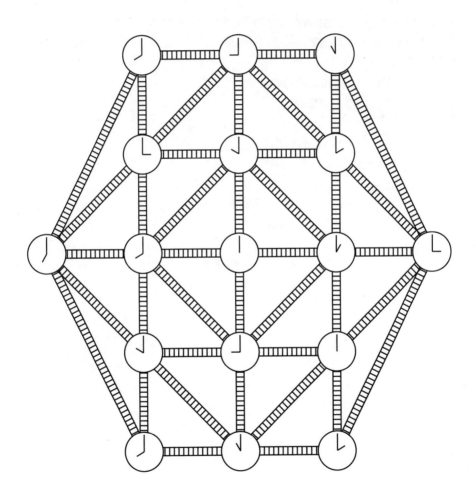

7. WHAT AM I?

My first is in **LEAVE**
But isn't in **LATE**.

My second is in **TIED**
But isn't in **DATE**.

My third is in **SEAT**
But isn't in **TEST**.

My fourth is in **DOOR**
But isn't in **REST**.

My fifth is in **RUST**
But isn't in **STORE**.

My sixth is in **CHEER**
But isn't in **SHORE**.

My seventh is in **MEET**
But isn't in **MORE**.

What am I?

8. CONNECTIONS

A vital part of any rail system is to have connections that allow you to change trains and move on to different routes.

In each case, find a railway word that connects the two given words below. The answer must link to the end of the first word and go in front of the second word.

I GOODS(_ _ _ _)ARM

2 FOOT(_ _ _ _ _ _)ROLL

3 RULE(_ _ _ _)STAND

4 HAND(_ _ _ _ _ _)BOX

5 RAFFLE(_ _ _ _ _ _)OFFICE

9. QUOTA

Solve the clues and put your answers in the correct squares in the grid. All answers have eight letters, unless we tell you otherwise. When the upper grid is complete the first column reading down will reveal the name of an author. Transfer the key-coded letters to the lower grid and complete a quotation by him, which reveals his secret as to how to be sure of catching a train.

I   A railway passenger vehicle.

2   Vacations, which were more common due to the railways of this era.

3   They were taken to safety via Operation Pied Piper in 1939.

4   Famous LNER express train, the *Flying* _____.

5   Stands on wheels for transporting luggage.

6   Locomotives which were neither steam nor diesel.

7   A busy 60 minutes of the day, morning or evening (4,4).

8   Leisure travellers, not business commuters.

9   This word goes before peak and after set (3) / Reserve a place (4).

10 Complex railway systems.

A B C D E F G H

(10×8 grid, rows 1–10, with a filled black square at D9)

D4	F7	■		F4	E8	H3	H10	■		C10	D7	H1	■
E6	D8	F2	E1	H4	■		E9	F3	C9	B2	F6	F5	

10. SINGLE TRACK

On a single-track railway, the down train and the up train share the same stretch of line.

This puzzle is just the same.

Answer the clues below, writing a single letter between each pair of sleepers, so that the letters work for both the down train clues and the up train clues. Down train answers read downwards and the up train answers read upwards. The arrows next to the track indicate the starting point of each answer.

We have given you the number of letters in each answer with each clue.

When you have all the answers in place, take the letters in the shaded spaces and arrange them to spell out the codename of a famous operation in the Second World War that involved the railway network. (Two words, 4 and 5 letters)

▼ DOWN TRAIN

Role in a play (**4**)

Male sheep (**3**)

Spoken (**4**)

Lives of a cat (**4**)

Force, strength (**5**)

High-pitched electronic sound (**5**)

UP TRAIN ▲

Orange skin (**4**)

Make beer (**4**)

Not closed (**4**)

Large Asian country (**5**)

Well dressed, neat (**5**)

A sharp blow (**3**)

▼ DOWN TRAIN

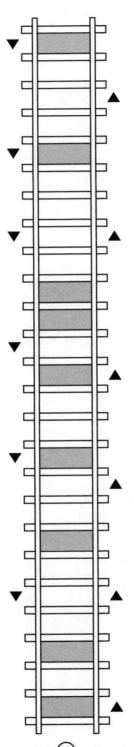

UP TRAIN ▲

11. CIRCULAR TOUR

Four stations are all linked on a circular loop line. The train starts at Northfields, then moves in a clockwise circular route calling at Eastfields, followed by Southfields, then Westfields, then back to Northfields and round again.

Charles is the only person to get on an early-morning train as it starts the first journey of the day from Northfields.

On the first circular trip one person gets on at each station on the route.

Someone has got off at every station as the train calls at Eastfields for a second time.

Valerie made the longest journey, going three stops.

Peter was the only person to travel one stop and he got off the train as Elizabeth got on.

Where did everyone get on and off?

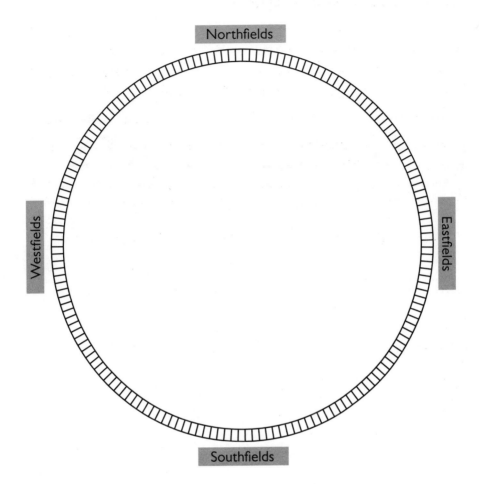

Northfields

Westfields

Eastfields

Southfields

Rearrange the letters to spell out the name of a station.

13. RESTRICTIONS

From the very beginning of railways there has been the constant need to maintain the tracks. Speed restrictions are often put in place when such work is carried out.

There is a 10-mile area of track where the speed is restricted to 30 miles per hour – 5 miles before the restricted area and 5 miles from leaving it, the train is allowed to travel at 60 miles per hour.

What is the average speed of the train as it covers this 20 miles of track?

14. ALL CHANGE

All change, please!

Rearrange the letters in each clue to make a new word with a railway connection.

The new word answers slot into the crossword-style grid and must link together.

ACROSS

7 Tear (4)

8 Credit (6)

10 Reserve (7)

11 Amend (5)

12 Send (4)

13 Liars (5)

17 Outer (5)

18 Neil (4)

22 Cedar (5)

23 Section (7)

24 Inn lad (6)

25 Fear (4)

DOWN

1 Bard ode (7)

2 I proved (7)

3 Tarts (5)

4 Gin lass (7)

5 Meats (5)

6 Dusty (5)

9 Predating (9)

14 Old gain (7)

15 Clerics (7)

16 Disease (7)

19 I rant (5)

20 Laces (5)

21 Mates (5)

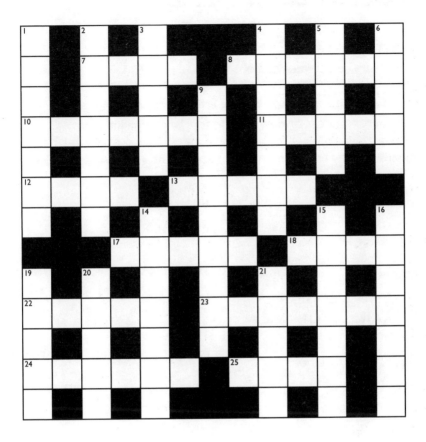

15. FULL SPEED AHEAD

There was fierce competition between companies to run the quickest passenger service between stations.

See if you are up to speed to fit all the listed words back into the frame. Words can read across or down and letters link at the junctions.

One word is in the list but cannot be placed in the grid. Which word is it?

3 Letters
ACE   GWR   RUN   VIA

4 Letters
BEST   CHUG   EDGE   FAST
PASS   RAIL   STOP   VIEW

5 Letters
CLIMB   FIRST   GUARD
HALTS   HILLS   SHUNT
SLOPE   SMOKE   TESTS

6 Letters
ASCENT   LONDON

7 Letters
COASTAL   EN ROUTE
EXPRESS   GLASGOW
PAPYRUS

8 Letters
STATIONS   VIADUCTS

9 Letters
EDINBURGH

10 Letters
PADDINGTON   SILVER LINK

11 Letters
CITY OF TRURO   THE PALATINE

12 Letters
BUILTH CASTLE

13 Letters
PRINCESS ROYAL

14 Letters
CORONATION SCOT
FLYING SCOTSMAN

15 Letters
CHELTENHAM FLYER

16 Letters
DOMINION OF CANADA

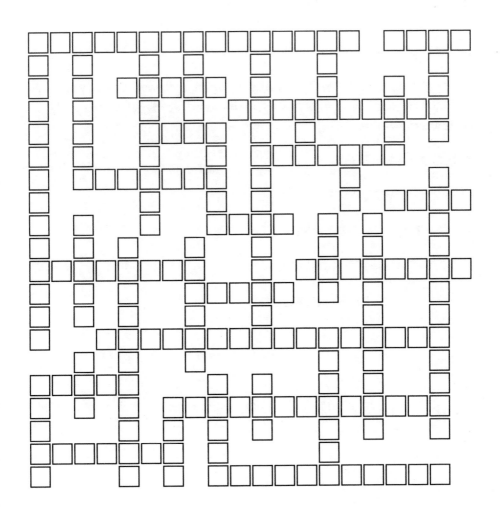

16. **SPLITS**

Carriages often split from the main train at various junctions en route.

In each of the groups below two words of equal length with a railway link are split into two, although the letters are in the correct order chronologically. What are the words?

1 COMAEACLHS

2 DSIRIVDINERG

3 BUENFGFIENET

4 DPIOERSETERL

5 RSIETNURGLEN

17. WHO IS IT?

Look at the three statements below. Consider yourself:

FIRST CLASS if you identify the fictional mystery personality and one of their novels after the first statement.

SECOND CLASS if you are correct after the second.

THIRD CLASS if you need all three statements to reveal **WHO IS IT?**

1   She first appeared as a character in a novel at the age of 74.

2   A friend of hers witnesses a murder on a train.

3   The train in the title of the novel had left a west London station around tea time.

18. SEASIDE SHUFFLE

The development of the railways in the first half of the 20th century played its part in making travel easier to coastal locations around Britain which then became popular holiday resorts.

Famous seaside names have had their letters mixed up and rearranged in alphabetical order. Unscramble the letters, find the names and work out their location on the map of Britain.

I BGHINORT

2 ABCEEMMOR

3 ACEENNPZ

4 EEGKNSSS

5 DEHNOSTU

19. BRIEF ENCOUNTER

At Milford Junction station a chance meeting in the refreshment room, between a doctor and a lady returning from a day's shopping, leads to a classic piece of cinema. Directed by David Lean, based on a one-act play by Noël Coward and with a music score by Rachmaninoff, *Brief Encounter* couldn't go wrong! Much of the film was shot at Carnforth station, which has become a Heritage Station and an essential destination for fans of the film and steam trains.

Find the words below in the letter grid. They are all in straight lines and can go across, backwards, up, down or diagonally.

CAKES	RAILWAY
CARRIAGE	REFRESHMENT ROOM
CHAIRS	SAUCER
CLOCK	SCONES
COMPARTMENT	SEAT
CUP	SHADOW
GUARD	STATION
JUG	SUBWAY
LIGHT	TABLES
LOCOMOTIVES	TEAPOT
LUNCH	TEAS
MIST	TELEPHONE
PASSENGERS	TICKET INSPECTOR
PLATES	TRAIN
PLATFORM	WAITRESS
	WINDOW

```
T X S S E V I T O M O C O L M
I L R R Z Q U L T R A A B O R
C U I E W O D A H S N R O A O
K N A G G L E Z S R A R W J F
E C H N H S N E S I T I O S T
T H C E B T R E L N N A C A A
I T W S L T T W E D E G L U L
N Y R S I A A M O X M E O C P
S A H A L Y H W G O T D C E S
P W W P I S V U D S R T K R T
E B O N E N J R C A A G C E A
C U W R O K A O U B P S A E T
T S F I L J N G L G M P K C I
O E L I T E L E P H O N E H O
R A M I S T S Z B T C D S P N
```

20. MILEAGE MATCH

Look at these rail journeys between famous stations and see if you can match them to the miles of track between them.

1   London Liverpool Street to Ipswich

2   Manchester Piccadilly to Liverpool Lime Street

3   Aberdeen to Inverness

4   Wolverhampton to Portsmouth Harbour

5   Swansea to Bangor (Gwynedd)

a) 31   **b)** 111   **c)** 83   **d)** 64   **e)** 131

21. WHAT'S THE LINK?

Rail travel is all about linking one station to another. Look at the three words below. Three words that have a common link can complete each one. What's the link?

1 BURN

2 CAR

3 HAVEN

22. STATIONGRAM

Rearrange the letters to spell out the name of a station.

RAT HOG EAR

23. MYSTERY OBJECT

Look at the **THREE** statements below and try to identify the mystery object.

If you get the answer after three clues award yourself a **SINGLE TICKET**.

If you get the answer after two clues award yourself a **RETURN TICKET**.

If you get the answer after one clue award yourself a **SEASON TICKET**!

1   It was designed by Sir Nigel Gresley in 1935.

2   It shares a name with a dabbling duck.

3   In July 1938 it reached 126mph, which was then a world speed record for a steam locomotive.

24. QUIZ TRAIN

All aboard to answer some quick-fire quiz clues!

ACROSS

3 The harbour station at which Kent Channel port closed in 1927? (5)

7 The Quintinshill rail disaster of 1915 happened near which 'Green' destination for runaway couples? (6)

8 Which Devon city did the *ACE* travel to after Sidmouth and Exmouth? (6)

10 Which town near Windsor had a railway run by GWR? (10)

11 The station for this independent school is south of the Thames (4)

12 Establish (3,2)

13 Breaks in one's journey (9)

16 Those of GWR locomotives were green framed with red (7)

21 Heading for Essex, Suffolk and Norfolk from London (9)

22 Inexpensive (5)

23 Border (4)

24 LMS record breaker the _____*Scot* (10)

26 Impact, such as the sparks _____ linked to house building and railways (6)

27 LNER locomotives *Link* and *Fox* (6)

28 Enclosed grounds attached to depots or stations (5)

DOWN

1 Oiled, lubricated (7)

2 Sporting arena, such as the one near Wembley Hill station (7)

3 The start of a new era (4)

4 Do this with a book, newspaper or magazine on your journey (4)

5 Book an exclusive seat (7)

6 Diversions (7)

9 Part of England served by GWR (4,7)

14 Coastal railway destination such as Southampton or Liverpool (4)

15 A series of junctions north of Birmingham New Street – not a London area for nightlife! (4)

17 Welsh terminus of Britain's first long-distance, high-speed diesel train service (7)

18 Guided (7)

19 This rail service goes back and forth over a short route (7)

20 This lady was awarded the George Medal for her actions during a GWR incident at sea (3,4)

24 GWR locomotive _____ of *Truro* (4)

25 Monstrous Scottish loch, accessed courtesy of LMS and LNER (4)

25. BOOKSTALL

The year 1848 saw the first station bookstall but by the end of the century there were around 1,000 all over the country.

Look at the clues below and work out the identity of an author and her novel, which is a classic of children's literature.

1   The story was originally serialised in *The London Magazine* in 1905 and was published as a book a year later.

2   Important characters include an Old Gentleman, who is a daily passenger on the 9.15, and the station porter Albert Perks.

3   The story tells of three children, Bobbie, Peter and Phyllis Waterbury, who moved from London to a house called The Three Chimneys in Yorkshire.

26. MEMORY TEST

—— URGENT NOTICE ——

PLEASE DO NOT LOOK AT THE QUESTIONS
BELOW. GO TO THE COLOUR PLATE
ON PAGE 9. STUDY THE POSTER FOR 2
MINUTES, THEN RETURN AND ANSWER
THE QUESTIONS BELOW FROM MEMORY.

1   Which London railway station is stated on the poster?

2   What type of locomotive is mentioned?

3   How long does it take to travel to Leeds?

4   How many serviettes are there on the table front left?

5   On the right of the poster, is the waiter serving a gentleman or a lady?

6   Which two Yorkshire destinations on the poster have five letters?

7   What type of carriage is shown in the poster?

8   The poster is called *Express Ease*; what colour is the lettering?

9   What can you see from the left-hand window – hills or houses?

10   Which is the most northerly destination mentioned on the poster?

Section Four

RETREAT AND REVIVAL

BRITAIN'S RAILWAYS
1951–PRESENT

Following nationalisation in 1948, the early years of British Railways were characterised by drift, muddle and upheaval, growing road competition and a severe lack of investment. The various levels of management lacked a clear structure, creating tension between the British Transport Commission and Railway Executive, as well as between the Executive and regional management.[1] As a result, the new Conservative government, elected in 1951, passed the Transport Act of 1953, which abolished the Railway Executive and denationalised much of the Road Haulage Executive. Following discussions with the government, the Commission published its 'Modernisation Plan' in January 1955. The plan stemmed from the belief that a '... modern well-equipped railway system is indispensable for the future of the country as a leading industrial power', and the need for modernisation was not lost on outside observers.[2] Correspondence published in the *Financial Times* in 1953 noted that British Railways' '... staffing and labour systems are obviously based on ideas which had to be abandoned years ago in industry'.[3] The plan used calculations made by the Executive, which envisaged a £500 million (over £14 billion at nominal 2019 prices) government investment loan, to be repaid through anticipated labour and cost savings. However, the Commission revised the Executive's loan estimate upwards to over £1.2 billion (nearly £34 billion at nominal 2019 prices), given the improvements that needed to be made. The areas for investment included 900 miles of new electrification projects, electric signalling and investment in freight services.[4]

Although the government underwrote the plan, it did little to check the financial details and it ultimately failed to stem British Railways' falling income.[5] In the case of freight, a failure to appreciate traffic trends meant that money was spent on unprofitable or inefficient services.[6] Similarly, an initial trial of different types of diesel locomotive to gradually replace steam degenerated into British Railways making panic orders from 1957; untested designs were bought off the drawing board while the purchase of a wide range of passenger diesel units from different manufacturers caused operational difficulties.[7] By the time the Modernisation Plan was stopped by the government in 1960, 2,239 diesel locomotives, 3,767 diesel multiple units and 246,882 wagons had been built, while steam locomotive construction ended the same year when a heavy-freight locomotive, No. 92220 *Evening Star*, was completed at Swindon.[8] However, the appointment of Dr Richard Beeching in 1961 as British Transport Commission chairman by the transport minister, Ernest Marples, marked the point at which British Railways would come to terms with the financial consequences of competition from other forms of transport.

A Change in Direction

Beeching was a physicist with little previous experience in transport but he was chosen for his track record in examining an organisation and taking action to achieve efficiencies and reduce costs.[9] Beeching increased the amount of data collected on the network's use to establish which services should be developed or dropped in the light of more general access to road transport.[10] A new Transport Act was passed in 1962 to create a British Railways Board with terms of reference that included the need to ensure that profits from operations should meet all running costs. It therefore granted the Board the same commercial freedom as road hauliers to seek the most profitable traffic, while unprofitable railway routes could be cut through accelerated closure procedures.[11]

These measures prepared the ground for two reports that were published to tackle the problem of British Railways' spiralling costs and falling income. These were *The Reshaping of British Railways* report of 1963, which controversially proposed that about a third of Britain's railway network should be closed to cut costs; and *The Development of the Major Railway Trunk Routes* of 1965, which proposed targeted investment to improve income from remaining services. This included the development of long-distance 'Liner Trains' with demountable containers capable of being transferred between rail and road; and the creation of 'Merry-Go-Round' short-distance coal trains, all underpinned by a complete overhaul of the organisation's image, which saw the emergence of the 'British Rail' brand.[12] One Modernisation Plan-era project that survived these changes was the phased electrification of the West Coast Main Line to link Crewe with Manchester and Liverpool; this was later extended to London Euston in 1965, Birmingham in 1967 and eventually to Glasgow in 1974. Electrification provided the cleaner, higher-speed, long-distance passenger services that were characteristic of the Inter-City brand introduced by British Rail in 1966. The rolling-out of diesel traction elsewhere meant that British Railways' steam locomotive fleet was gradually withdrawn from service, and the end finally came in August 1968. Aside from official preservation, many steam locomotives were purchased from a South Wales scrapyard and restored to working order for use on Britain's Heritage Railways, which had been growing in number since the opening of the volunteer-run narrow-gauge Talyllyn Railway in 1951.[13]

Although line closures continued under successive Labour and Conservative governments, the 1970s saw moves towards improving network use. British Rail made increasing use of computer technology and electronics to collect and process information as well as automate previously labour-intensive processes. This included the adoption of the American-designed Total Operations Processing System (TOPS) from 1973. The system enabled analysis of freight services to achieve better utilisation of existing equipment, thereby saving money on locomotive and rolling stock purchases and aiding train planning.[14] Another innovation of the period was the Advanced Passenger Train project, which sought to increase train speeds on existing lines without the need for costly re-engineering. However, its prolonged development spurred a stopgap – the High Speed Diesel Train – with an operating speed of 125 miles per hour and, although the Advanced Passenger Train was ultimately cancelled, the High Speed Train proved a marketing sensation by providing a regular high-speed service for all passengers on non-electrified routes from 1976. Such was the success of the High Speed Train concept that many remain in service in the 2020s.

New Challenges, New Opportunities

The 1980s, however, was a challenging decade for the railways; financial pressures facing the government reduced the likelihood of investment and an economic recession severely hit British Rail's income, prompting the management to examine various solutions including the sale of redundant assets and cost-cutting through service reductions and closures. An example was the former Great Central Railway line between Sheffield and Manchester, which had closed to passengers in 1970 and was completely closed in 1981 despite being electrified in 1953, the reasons being route duplication and the incompatibility of the electrical system with those parts of the network electrified during the 1960s. In 1982, passenger numbers had reached their lowest level for the 20th century, while proposed changes to various aspects of British Rail's business eroded industrial relations.[15] A report by David Serpell on the state of British Rail recommended that the organisation should live within its means, with various options suggested for achieving this end. The option that gained notoriety suggested an 84 per cent reduction in the network to 1,630 miles, with main lines centred on the London–Cardiff, Newcastle and Glasgow routes.[16]

While the report was shelved, more closures were considered; a 1984 proposal for the Settle–Carlisle line was vehemently opposed, and the route was reprieved five years later. Ancillary activities such as shipping, cross-Channel hovercraft and hotels were sold into private ownership, while British Rail moved away from a regionally based management structure controlling all activities to one split between individual services, or sectors.[17] Sectorisation marked the transition towards privatising British Rail; the Conservative government sought to reduce spending by returning publicly owned assets to the private sector. This is perhaps best shown by the major infrastructure project of the era, the Channel Tunnel linking the railway networks of Britain and France, which was undertaken by private enterprise.[18] The Railways Act of 1993 authorised the privatisation of British Rail the following year, beginning the process of separating the ownership of trains and track, with firms awarded franchises to run passenger services on the rails of a shareholder-funded national infrastructure owner – Railtrack.[19]

Relying upon sub-contractors for maintenance, Railtrack was liquidated in 2001 following a string of accidents, at Southall, Ladbroke Grove and Hatfield. In addition, a decline in service reliability due to worn infrastructure brought accusations that the organisation had not been giving track maintenance and renewal the attention they deserved.[20] Consequently, ownership of railway infrastructure passed to publicly owned Network Rail.[21] This organisation has since overseen the expansion of the railway network in Scotland, while several electrification projects are underway across the country. Some are timely – environmental concerns and traffic congestion have revitalised public interest in the railways as an alternative form of transport, bringing profound passenger growth. However, delay, cancellation and overcrowding on passenger services remain perennial issues, and the gradual replacement of ageing former British Rail rolling stock continues into the 2020s. The new millennium has seen discussion turn towards augmenting the railway network with high-speed rail to increase capacity, although the expense and necessity are hotly debated. Regardless, Britain's railways have come a long way from the horse-drawn wooden waggonway. The constant stream of innovations and new approaches means there is little sign of them standing still for years to come.

1. TRAINSPOTTING

The 1940s and 50s were seen as the golden age of trainspotting. Young and old up and down the country gathered on stations to record the numbers of locomotives that passed through. Willesden Junction closed its doors to trainspotters in 1954. It was estimated that this affected up to half a million trainspotting enthusiasts.

In this grid we want you to spot a train number in a different way. There's no need to hang around a station! Fill in the grid below so that the digits 1–9 appear in each row, each column and each 3 x 3 square. When the grid is complete take the letters in the shaded squares, reading left to right top to bottom to reveal the number of a famous locomotive. It was given a name that was previously the nickname of another famous engine.

	9		5		7		8	
		1	8		4	9		
8								6
		9		7		2		
		3		2		6		
			1		5			
3								5
		7	3		2	1		
	2		4		6		3	

2. DRONE RANGER

Two railway stations are exactly 60 miles apart. At exactly the same time a train leaves each station. Both trains are travelling at a constant speed of 60 miles per hour and both are non-stopping services.

A drone sets off from station A with the task of scanning the track throughout the journey. The drone is travelling at 70 miles per hour, so it soon leaves the train from station A behind. It carries on until it meets the train from station B heading down the track on its journey to station A.

The drone turns around and follows the direction of train B. The quicker-moving drone leaves train B behind and eventually meets up with train A. The drone turns around once more. This happens again and again, until the two trains meet each other on their respective tracks.

How far had the drone travelled when the two trains meet?

3. THE BEECHING AXE

Dr Richard Beeching was chairman of British Rail in the 1960s when 5,000 miles of track and over 2,000 stations were axed from the railway network.

Here's an ABC list of some of the stations that were closed down. This is your chance to get them back on track by fitting all the names into the frame. Words can go across or down and interlock where tracks cross. The name **BEECHING** also appears, and we start you off with a piece of **TRACK** to get going.

4 Letters

BALA

5 Letters

APPIN	AYTON	BACUP
BANFF	BLABY	CALNE
CARNO	CLARE	TRACK

7 Letters

ASHCOTT   CREAGAN

8 Letters

ABERBRAN	ABINGDON
ACREFAIR	BAKEWELL
BALLATER	BEECHING
CARDIGAN	COVE HALT

9 Letters

ALDEBURGH
CAVENDISH
CHATTERIS

10 Letters

BROAD CLYST

12 Letters

CULLODEN MOOR

13 Letters

BRIGHTLINGSEA
COALBROOKDALE

14 Letters

BLANDFORD FORUM

17 Letters

BUDLEIGH SALTERTON

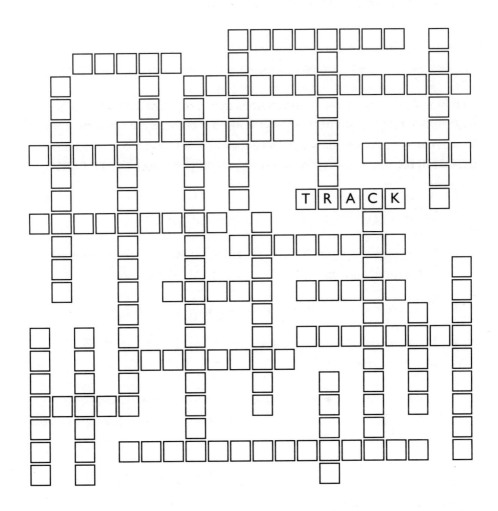

4. RAILWAYANIA

Railway memorabilia has developed into big business, with many specialist auctions held for the thousands of enthusiasts who are on the lookout to collect anything linked to the history of railways.

At an auction it so happens that the first five items for sale are all different types of object. They all have a different market value and they came to their owners from a different source. Use the clues to piece the information together.

1   The box of timetables had the lowest value at £20.

2   The station clock that is valued at £500 has 10 times the market value of the item found in the loft.

3   The poster, which was a gift, is valued twice as much as the lamp.

4   The item with the highest value, £1,000, was bought by the present owner at an auction.

5   The item acquired from the family was less valuable than the item picked up at a charity sale. The enamel sign was not acquired in either of these ways.

What was each item valued at and how had their owners come to acquire them?

5. STATIONGRAM

Rearrange the letters to spell out the name of a station. There are two words.

6. A to Z

This puzzle looks like an ordinary crossword. However, there are no clues. The letters A to Z are each represented by a number instead. We have given you the numbers that represent the letters in the word **CLASS** to start you off. Most answers are made up of a single word, but also look out for two words that are coupled together!

The checklist below will help you to keep track of the letters you have found.

1 = **C**, 2 = **L**, 3 = **A**, 4 = **S**,

5 = , 6 = , 7 = , 8 = , 9 = , 10 = , 11 = , 12 = , 13 = , 14 = , 15 = , 16 = , 17 = , 18 = , 19 = , 20 = , 21 = , 22 = , 23 = , 24 = , 25 = , 26 =

When you have filled in the crossword and worked out all the letters, look at the numbers below and find the name of a British Prime Minister, who as a director of **GWR** had the privilege of first-**CLASS** travel on the British rail network.

8 3 12 11 2 20

21 3 1 21 19 2 2 3 5

7. HIDDEN FINDS

Twenty-first century trains are very different from their early 19th-century ancestors. Words that would not have been part of rail vocabulary more than a century and a half ago are hidden in each of the sentences below. Discover them by linking words or parts of words together.

1   I will follow if I can discover the best way ahead.

2   The elderly lady needed help lugging her suitcase along the platform.

3   Smelling cheap perfume can be quite an unpleasant experience.

4   The popular CD, also known as a compact disc, re-entered the classical charts this week.

5   We found the material apt, operational and suited to our needs.

8. BOOKSTALL

In 1905 station owners threatened to raise the rent on station bookstalls. W.H. Smith decided to purchase retail properties in roads that conveniently led to stations. This meant that when Dr Beeching wielded the axe that closed many stations, the shops did not need to close.

Look at the clues below and work out the identity of an author and the first of her highly successful series of novels.

1 The author also writes crime fiction under the pseudonym Robert Galbraith.

2 The Express train that serves the school in the novels leaves from Kings Cross, at the beginning of every term heading for Hogsmeade station.

3 Cauldron cakes can be bought from the trolley on the train.

9. ENGINE RESTORATION

Five Heritage Railway enthusiasts each rent a shed in a work yard in order to restore a vintage engine back to its former glory. Each one has a keen interest in an engine with a particular wheel arrangement and spends a different number of hours per week on their pet project.

By looking at the plan and studying the information below, can you work out where each enthusiast's shed is located, which type of engine they specialise in and how many hours per week they spend there? When you find a piece of positive information, put a tick in the appropriate box in the upper grid. Put a cross when you discover a piece of negative information.

Cross-refer so that you can complete the lower grid.

1 Joe's shed abuts two other sheds. He is restoring a 2-8-2 engine.

2 The person restoring the 0-6-2 spends half the number of hours in his shed as the person who is restoring a 4-6-2 in shed B.

3 Ken, in shed D, is not the person who spends ten hours a week on a 2-2-2.

4 Mike, who spends the most time on restoration work, has the shed with most interior walls.

5 Andrew's shed does not abut the shed where the owner spends 14 hours each week.

Logic Grid Puzzle

		Shed					Hours/Week					Wheel Arrangement				
		A	B	C	D	E	8 hours	10 hours	14 hours	16 hours	20 hours	0-6-2	2-2-2	2-8-2	4-4-0	4-6-2
Name	Andrew															
	Graham															
	Joe															
	Ken															
	Mike															
Wheel Arrangement	0-6-2															
	2-2-2															
	2-8-2															
	4-4-0															
	4-6-2															
Hours/Week	8 hours															
	10 hours															
	14 hours															
	16 hours															
	20 hours															

Shed Floorplan

A	B
C	D
	E

Name	Shed	Hours/Week	Wheel Arrangement

10. HERITAGE

Heritage Railways are often old railway lines that have been preserved or restored to give those who live in the 21st century a glimpse into the history of this much-loved mode of transport.

Famous Heritage Railways have had their letters mixed up below and rearranged in alphabetical order. Can you unscramble the letters, find the names and work out their location on the map of Britain?

1 BBEELLLU

2 ADMOORRT

3 ADDILMN

4 AACDEILNNO

5 AEGLLLLNNO

Express Ease (c1925) features artwork by George Harrison, and shows the interior of the restaurant car of the London and North Eastern Railway's 'Harrogate Pullman' service. Beginning in July 1923, the train linked Kings Cross with Leeds, Harrogate and Ripon, before travelling onwards to Darlington and Newcastle.

Women locomotive cleaners at Bradford Low Moor, March 1917. Military conscription created vacancies across the railway business, and the first women locomotive cleaners were employed in 1916. Women were recruited to male roles from 1915 and faced prejudice from management, railwaymen and trade unions alike.

Coronation Scot Ascending Shap Fell (1937) features artwork by Norman Wilkinson. It showcases the London, Midland and Scottish Railway's new train hauled by its new 'Princess Coronation' Class. Along with the London and North Eastern Railway's A4s of 1935, these locomotives were potent symbols of streamlining, speed and power in Britain, helping to sell the service during economic uncertainty.

Bomb damage at St Pancras (May 1941). The Second World War brought a new threat to the railways – intensive aerial bombardment. London's railways were badly affected, although few important railway hubs were beyond a bomber's range. Men and women laboured day and night in difficult conditions to make bomb-damaged lines operational.

Shabby? (1945) was issued by the Southern Railway and uses artwork by L. A. Webb. The railways emerged from the Second World War tired and needing investment, and there were plans to take this in hand. However, the political debate had shifted towards bringing the railways into public ownership. They were nationalised in 1948 to create British Railways.

Evening Star naming ceremony New main-line steam locomotives continued to be built until 1960 and the last, Class 9F No. 92220 *Evening Star*, is pictured during its naming ceremony at Swindon Works. Although steam locomotives remained the main form of traction for nearly two decades of British Railways' existence, the 'Modernisation Plan' of 1955 had begun the process of replacing steam with diesel and electric.

London Midland Electrification (1963) features artwork by John Greene and shows progress on the West Coast Main Line electrification scheme at Stafford. This long-term project was authorised under the 1955 Modernisation Plan, and despite general cutbacks in investment, the electrification of the entire route between London and Glasgow was complete by 1974.

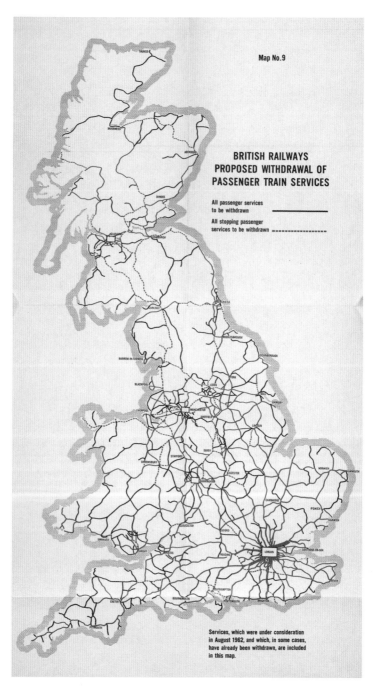

Map No.9

BRITISH RAILWAYS
PROPOSED WITHDRAWAL OF
PASSENGER TRAIN SERVICES

All passenger services
to be withdrawn _____

All stopping passenger
services to be withdrawn ....

Services, which were under consideration
in August 1962, and which, in some cases,
have already been withdrawn, are included
in this map.

British Railways map Richard Beeching, the new chairman of the British Transport Commission, was asked to produce a report, *The Reshaping of British Railways*, to create a self-sustaining network to address falling income and rising costs. Published in 1963, it controversially proposed the closure of approximately a third of the network, as this map indicates. Many closures were carried out over the following decade.

Look what you gain when you travel by train

Now: London to Bath, a comfortable 69 minutes

Now: London to Bristol Temple Meads, a smooth 85 minutes

Now: London to Cardiff, a relaxing 105 minutes

Now: London to Swansea, an easy 163 minutes

Pick up a free copy of the pocket timetable

Inter-City 125 makes the going easy

Look What You Gain When You Travel By Train (1977) depicts British Rail's new High Speed Train, introduced in 1976 as a stopgap during the prolonged development of the Advanced Passenger Train. The poster highlights the acceleration of services on the former Great Western Main Line out of Paddington.

This is the age of the train ⥮

left

The Shape of Travel to Come (c1980) illustrates a pre-production Advanced Passenger Train, which used tilting technology to counter the constraints preventing high-speed running on the West Coast Main Line. Despite prolonged development, the project was eventually abandoned in the mid-1980s. Tilting technology would later return to the West Coast Main Line with the Class 390 Pendolino trains.

below

Eurostar The Channel Tunnel was built to connect Britain with mainland Europe, and the Class 373 *Eurostar* was developed to run on the different power supplies encountered on the railways of western Europe. Eurostar services began in 1994, and it is possible to travel from London St Pancras to Paris Gare du Nord in just over two hours.

II. KEEPING TRACK

New Street has 25 platforms and a train arriving or departing every 37 seconds.

It's a highly complex task to monitor the movements of vehicles by studying real-time screen plans in the control room.

Our plan shows the tracks leaving four platforms at Old Street station, together with the stations that are located along the routes. From which platform do trains depart to New Street station and how many stations are there en route?

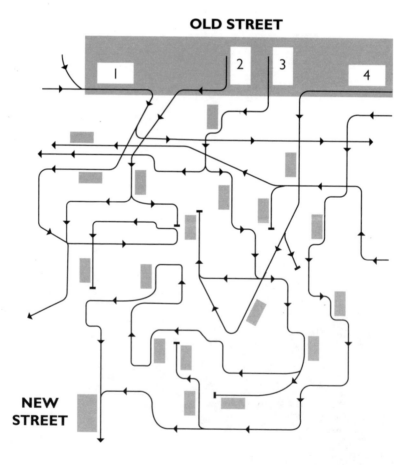

12. SPLITS

Carriages often split from the main train at various junctions en route.

In each of the groups of letters below, two words of equal length with a railway link are split into two, although the letters are in the correct order chronologically. What are the words?

1 FSHARUENST

2 DEGOOPOTDS

3 CTHIANCGKETE

4 BASTRATIRIEONR

5 FRESEIRVIGCHTE

13. QUOTA

Solve the clues and put your answers in the correct squares in the grid. All answers have eight letters unless we indicate otherwise. When the upper grid is complete the first column reading down will reveal the name of an author. Transfer the key-coded letters to the lower grid and complete a quotation by him.

1 Station that was the original London terminus for Channel Tunnel trains.

2 Great Western Railway is also known by the _____ GWR.

3 Midday meals, popular in buffet cars. (7)

4 Suitcases, bags, briefcases, hatboxes etc. (7)

5 Internal system to connect people via radio or telephone.

6 Software program used on an electronic device and containing a travel ticket for example (3) / Concourse or large area at a station. (4)

7 A principal railway route. (4,4)

8 'A' stands for this in the abbreviation APT.

9 Signs of difficulties or dangers when travelling.

10 Transfer data from device to device such as travel information.

11 Pass that allows reduction in fares for students, seniors etc. on trains.

12 Home of the National Railway Museum (4) / Route chart. (3)

	A	B	C	D	E	F	G	H
1								
2								
3								■
4								■
5								
6				■				
7								
8								
9								
10								
11								
12					■			

B1	■	H2	C5	H7	D8	F12	■			
	■						■			
G4	C3	G9	C11	D10	D1	■	E6	F2	H9	■
						■				■
E4	D11	C10	B9	A12	G3	■	C4	G5	C1	■
						■				■
E11	E3	B7	E1	G10	F8	D2	D5	C9	■	
									■	

14. MYSTERY OBJECT

Look at the **THREE** statements below and try to identify the mystery object.

If you get the answer after three clues award yourself a **SINGLE TICKET**.

If you get the answer after two clues award yourself a **RETURN TICKET**.

If you get the answer after one clue award yourself a **SEASON TICKET**!

1   I cost 2 shillings in 1922.

2   I had a yellow cover.

3   A Railway Guide, my final issue was in 1961.

15. STATIONGRAM

Rearrange the letters to spell out the name of a station.

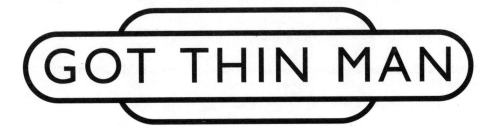

GOT THIN MAN

16. WHO IS IT?

Look at the three statements below. Consider yourself:

FIRST CLASS if you identify the mystery person after the first statement.

SECOND CLASS if you are correct after the second.

THIRD CLASS if you need all three statements to reveal **WHO IS IT?**

1   He appeared on TV as a child advertising a well-known blackcurrant drink.

2   Among his Parliamentary roles he was a Minister of State for Transport.

3   He has made many TV programmes about Great Railways Journeys, both in the UK and overseas.

17. WHAT AM I?

My first is in **CABLE**
But isn't in **PLACE**.

My second is in **RACES**
But isn't in **SPACE**.

My third is in **TIMES**
But isn't in **STEAM**.

My fourth is in **DATE**
But isn't in **TEAM**.

My fifth is in **GUARD**
But isn't in **CARD**.

My sixth is in **READY**
But isn't in **YARD**.

What am I?

18. SINGLE TRACK

On a single-track railway, the down train and the up train share the same stretch of line.

This puzzle is just the same.

Answer the clues below, writing a single letter between each pair of sleepers, so that the letters work for both the down train clues and the up train clues. Down train answers read downwards and the up train answers read upwards. The arrows next to the track indicate the starting point of each answer.

We have given you the number of letters in each answer with each clue.

When you have all the answers in place, take the letters in the shaded spaces to spell out the name of a famous station terminus from 1994 to 2007.

▼ DOWN TRAIN

They control water flow (**4**)

Also (**3**)

Ale (**4**)

Festive event (**4**)

Not a consonant (**5**)

Sweeping brush (**5**)

UP TRAIN ▲

Northern hill (**4**)

Make a sound through a whistle (**4**)

Egg shaped (**4**)

Concur (**5**)

Sturdy footwear (**5**)

Strike gently (**3**)

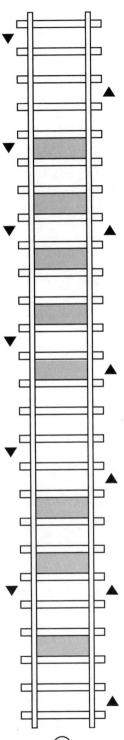

▼ **DOWN TRAIN**

UP TRAIN ▲

19. POINTS

Find a single three-letter railway-linked word that can go in front of all the letter groups on the tracks and create new words of six letters.

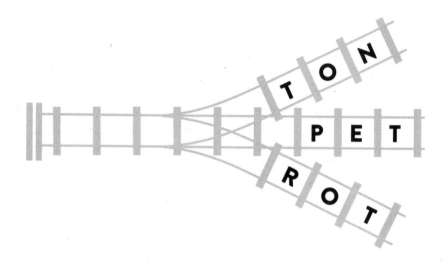

20. **A CLASS ACT**

Class numbers for locomotives are usually written as digits.

Digits can, of course, be written out as words using capital letters only. So, for example, Class 11 could be written as **ELEVEN**.

The individual letters can all be formed by using straight lines – **E** has four lines; **L** has two lines; as does **V**; **N** has three straight lines. The word **ELEVEN** has a total of **SEVENTEEN** straight lines.

What number, when its name is written down using capital letters, is composed of as many straight lines as the number itself? It is also the same number as a class of locomotives that operated in the 1960s.

21. CHANNEL TUNNEL

The idea of creating a Channel Tunnel was first suggested in the 18th century but it wasn't until the 20th century – 1994 to be exact – that the tunnel commenced operation. Find the words with a Channel Tunnel link below in the letter grid. They are all in straight lines and can go across, backwards, up, down or diagonally. To challenge you a little bit more, can you find which word appears not once but twice.

ASHFORD

CHERITON

CITY

CONNECTION

COQUELLES

DOVER

EBBSFLEET

EUROPE

EUROSTAR

FARES

FOLKESTONE

FRANCE

GREAT BRITAIN

KENT

LE SHUTTLE

LINK

LOGO

LONDON

PARIS

PAS DE CALAIS

PASSENGER

RAIL

RIDE

ROUTES

SEAT

SPEED

ST PANCRAS

TICKET

TRANSMANCHE

UNDERSEA

WIFI

```
G  X  E  L  T  T  U  H  S  E  L  C  R  C  S
I  R  L  B  Z  Q  R  O  U  T  E  S  A  O  T
W  U  E  I  B  O  P  A  H  C  X  S  I  Q  P
I  T  R  A  N  S  M  A  N  C  H  E  L  U  A
F  F  C  N  T  K  F  A  R  F  T  S  O  E  N
I  O  C  H  A  B  R  L  O  I  I  N  D  L  C
J  L  L  S  E  F  R  R  E  A  S  O  P  L  R
R  K  U  K  S  R  D  I  L  E  V  I  A  E  A
A  E  E  N  E  Y  I  A  T  E  T  T  S  S  S
T  S  N  D  S  C  T  R  A  T  C  S  I  P
S  T  S  O  T  E  T  I  O  L  I  E  E  X  D
O  O  E  E  D  I  R  O  T  N  C  N  N  A  E
R  N  R  S  J  N  G  S  N  Y  K  N  G  P  E
U  E  A  E  U  R  O  P  E  E  E  O  E  O  P
E  P  F  S  O  G  O  L  T  A  T  C  R  X  S
```

22. QUIZ TRAIN

All aboard to answer some quick-fire quiz clues!

ACROSS

3 Chocolate drink from the station buffet (5)

7 Tank for heating water on a Heritage Railway for example (6)

8 Collect from a station (4,2)

10 Puzzles to keep you amused on a long journey (10)

11 Writer Blyton whose *Famous Five* characters were used in a GWR marketing campaign (4)

12 Racecourse on the Waterloo to Reading line (5)

13 London terminal for Eurostar (2,7)

16 Levels of travel such as first or standard (7)

21 Means of travel (9)

22 Official in charge of a train (5)

23 Type of locomotive used in the *Harry Potter* films (4)

24 Carriers of postal items (4,6)

26 Comfortable waiting area for Eurostar (6)

27 Reserved (6)

28 Drop-down place for your lunch or your laptop (5)

DOWN

1 Leisure traveller (7)

2 Scottish terminus of Avanti West Coast trains (7)

3 Team who work together on a train (4)

4 Download these to buy tickets or access info (4)

5 Stephenson's *Puffing Billy* is now in this London museum (7)

6 *Starlight Express* is this form of theatre (7)

9 Organisation which owned the railways after nationalisation (7,4)

14 Chopped down, as with Dr Beeching's cuts to the rail network (4)

15 Detach a carriage from a moving train (4)

17 Innovator, designer (7)

18 Which country has the most westerly terminus of the Channel Tunnel? (7)

19 Keeper or custodian of a museum (7)

20 Labelled with a trademark, important during the Beeching era (7)

24 Come together at a station (4)

25 Nickname for part of London's metropolitan railway system (4)

23. **STATIONGRAM**

Rearrange the letters to spell out the name of a station.
There are two words.

24. HOME RUN

Every weekday thousands of people pack into busy trains as they leave their jobs in the cities and set off for their homes. An evening train sets off and the carriage is full. There are 10 stops in all, but after the fifth stop there are only five commuters remaining.

Each commuter has a different type of reading material and they all have different occupations.

One of the five gets out at each of the remaining stations on the line.

Using the clues below, try to name each person, give their occupation, say what they were reading and at which station they ended their rail journey.

CLUES

- Someone is reading text messages on a smart phone.

- Mr James was still on the train after Mrs Brown had got off. Neither of these was the newspaper reader.

- Mr Khan, a lawyer, did not get off at the seventh station. He was not the person who read a magazine and got off at the sixth station.

- One of the five reads a paperback novel, but this was neither Mr Wilson nor the accountant who both remained on the train as it pulled out of the station after the eighth stop.

- Mrs Patel, a secretary, was reading material on her laptop.

- One of the five people is a social worker.

- The person with the second longest commute was the librarian who got out at the ninth stop.

25. CONNECTIONS

A vital part of any rail system is to have connections that allow you to change trains and move on to different routes.

In each case, find a railway word that connects the two given words. The answer must link to the end of the first word and go in front of the second word.

  1 ROLLING(_ _ _ _ _)MARKET

    2 CHANNEL(_ _ _ _ _ _)VISION

      3 TIME(_ _ _ _ _)TENNIS

        4 HALF(_ _ _ _)WELL

          5 CUSTOMER(_ _ _ _ _ _ _)CHARGE

26. MEMORY TEST

URGENT NOTICE

PLEASE DO NOT LOOK AT THE QUESTIONS BELOW. GO TO THE COLOUR PLATE ON PAGE 15. STUDY THE POSTER FOR 2 MINUTES, THEN RETURN AND ANSWER THE QUESTIONS BELOW FROM MEMORY.

1   How many trains are there?

2   Are all the trains facing east or west?

3   Which city is the destination of the longest journey?

4   Which Welsh city beginning with 'C' is named on the poster?

5   What does the poster ask you to pick up a free copy of?

6   In the title of the poster which two different words rhyme?

7   Which number follows the words Inter-City?

8   The Inter-City 'double arrow' logo is white on the trains. What colour is it at the foot of the poster?

9   The shortest journey named has the shortest name of a destination. What is it?

10   Each journey is described differently as comfortable, smooth, relaxing and which other word?

THE SOLUTIONS

Puzzle 1: **INDUSTRIALISATION WORD SEARCH**

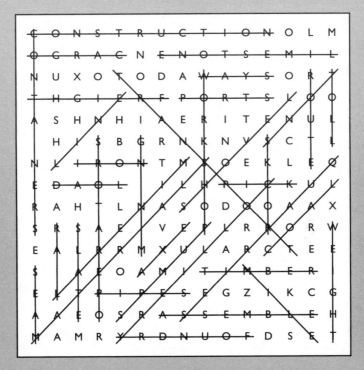

IRON appears twice.

Puzzle 2: **WHAT AM I?**

WAGON. The first letter is **W**. The second letter is an **A** or an **E**. The third letter is **G**. The fourth letter is an **O** or a **U**. The fifth letter is an **I** or an **N**. Wagon is the only word that can be formed by these options.

Puzzle 3: **ON TRIAL**

The difference between the top speed trial and the average speed trial would have been **1½ hours**. A single return trip is 3 miles so the total of 10 trips is 30 miles. At 30 miles per hour, the entire distance would have taken 1 hour. At 12 miles per hour the 30 miles would take 2½ hours to travel. That gives the difference of **1½ hours**.

Puzzle 4: **WAGGONWAY**

Puzzle 5: **A to Z**

The words reading **ACROSS** from left to right, top to bottom are:

Ravine, Quarries, Plan, Gates, Door, Raced, Passenger, Non stop, Direction, Trips, Flat, Metal, Took, Unloaded, Prizes.

The words reading **DOWN** from left to right, top to bottom are:

Wayleave, Pioneer, Weigh, Maps, Trading, Remote, Transport, Slow, Jolt, Explored, Section, Britain, Inland, Slope, Made.

1 = P, 2 = I, 3 = O, 4 = N, 5 = E, 6 = R, 7 = T, 8 = D, 9 = U, 10 = A, 11 = K, 12 = F, 13 = C, 14 = V, 15 = B, 16 = W, 17 = J, 18 = X, 19 = Z, 20 = Y, 21 = L, 22 = G, 23 = M, 24 = Q, 25 = S, 26 = H.

The letters that you find from the listed numbers spell out the name of railway pioneer **RICHARD TREVITHICK**.

Puzzle 6: **CONNECTIONS**

1 Wheel; **2** Iron; **3** Stop; **4** Mine; **5** Engine.

Puzzle 7: **MYSTERY OBJECT**

Coal

Puzzle 8: **ROCKET WHEEL**

1 Planet; **2** Engine; **3** Robert; **4** Shovel; **5** Emblem; **6** Valley; **7** Enters; **8** Record; **9** Ascent; **10** Narrow; **11** Corner; **12** Employ.

The perimeter of the wheel spells **PERSEVERANCE**, which is a locomotive by Timothy Burstall at the Rainhill Trials.

Puzzle 9: **SINGLE TRACK**

Down train: Boss; Pan; Sail; Axes; Sepal; Fires.

Up train: Serif; Lap; Essex; Alias; Naps; Sob.

The name of the steam locomotive is **SANS PAREIL**.

Puzzle 10: **QUOTA**

1 Whistles; **2** Engineer; **3** Labourer; **4** Lighting; **5** Inventor; **6** Nickname; **7** Gradient; **8** Terminus; **9** Operator; **10** Northern.

The Duke reading Down in the first column is **WELLINGTON**.

The quotation that gives the reason for his disapproval of the railways is because they '... **ENCOURAGE THE LOWER ORDERS TO TRAVEL ABOUT**'.

Puzzle 11: **SHAPE UP**

1 Rocket; **2** Cart; **3** Tracks; **4** Gates; **5** Carriages.

Puzzle 12: **ON THE MOVE**

1 Slate; **2** Coal; **3** Iron; **4** Stone; **5** Tin.

Puzzle 13: **GOODS YARD**

Puzzle 14: **WHO IS IT?**

The mystery personality is **Robert Stephenson**.

Puzzle 15: **PIONEERING PLACES**

1 Darlington; **2** Liverpool; **3** Manchester; **4** Rainhill; **5** Stockton.

On the map: Liverpool is the most westerly. The next dot to the east is Rainhill, while Manchester is the next dot east of that. The most easterly dot is Stockton, with Darlington to the west of that.

Puzzle 16: **QUIZ TRAIN**

ACROSS: **3** Wheel; **7** Remote; **8** Attend; **10** Directions; **11** Trip; **12** Slate; **13** Hackworth; **16** Waggons; **21** Liverpool; **22** Chalk; **23** Flue; **24** Signalling; **26** Handle; **27** Reopen; **28** Drive.

DOWN: **1** Vehicle; **2** Novelty; **3** West; **4** Laws; **5** Station; **6** *Invicta*; **9** *Royal George*; **14** Kent; **15** Lamp; **17** William; **18** Legends; **19** Shildon; **20** Planned; **24** Shed; **25** Acre.

Puzzle 17: **THE RAINHILL TRIALS**

Mr Andrews/Grocer/*Sans Pareil*/18mph
Mr Charles/Miner/*Novelty*/5mph
Mr George/Engineer/*Rocket*/20mph
Mr Henry/Seaman/*Perseverance*/10mph
Mr Ward/Farmer/*Cycloped*/15mph

Puzzle 18: **SIDINGS**

Grab a cuppa – this is a long answer!

The engine moves to **siding C**, then goes to couple **wagon 2**. The engine returns to its original position. **Wagon 2** is uncoupled. The engine moves in to **siding C** so that it can then move into **siding B**. **Wagon 1** is now moved for the first time as it is shunted into **siding A** where it is left.

The engine then moves **wagon 2** into **siding C**. The wagon is left there as the engine moves to **siding B**, and then back into **siding A** where it couples with **wagon 1**. Engine and wagon move into **siding C**, where **wagon 2** is also positioned. The engine moves **wagon 1** to the position where **wagon 2** started off.

The engine leaves **wagon 1** and moves back into **siding C**. The engine couples with **wagon 2** and then heads along the straight section of track and into **siding A**. **Wagon 2** is then moved round the bend heading to **siding B**, but is left in the position where **wagon 1** started. The two wagons are now in their final places.

The engine reverses back into **siding A**, and then heads down the straight section of track to reach its original position.

Puzzle 19: **WHEEL-WRITE**

   1 Signalled

   2 Pressures

   3 Cylinders

   The ? sign stands for a letter **E**.

Puzzle 20: **ROCKET ON**

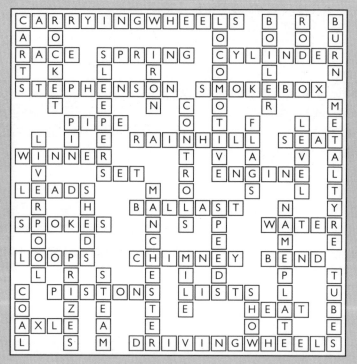

BUFFER is the word that is left over.

Puzzle 21: **SPLITS**

1 Coal/Iron

2 Steam/Wagon

3 Route/Works

4 Gauge/Track

5 Smoke/Wheel

Puzzle 22: **MEMORY TEST**

1 1825

2 LNER

3 *Locomotion*

4 George Stephenson

5 Two

6 Left

7 Top hat

8 Four

9 Man on the left

10 Our Centenary

SECTION TWO

Puzzle 1: **BOOKSTALL**

The author was **Charles Dickens** and the book was *Dombey and Son*.

Puzzle 2: **STATIONGRAM**

The station is **PITLOCHRY**.

Puzzle 3: **QUOTA**

1 Mailbags; **2** Inclines; **3** Stations; **4** Scottish; **5** Platform; **6** Reserved; **7** Isambard; **8** Shunting; **9** Murderer.

The character reading Down in the first column was **MISS PRISM**.

In the book she had left a baby in a handbag at **VICTORIA** railway station, which is **THE BRIGHTON LINE**.

Puzzle 4: **SINGLE TRACK**

Down train: Burn; Age; Brag; Used; After; Freed.

Up train: Deer; Fret; Fade; Sugar; Began; Rub.

The destination is **ABERDEEN**.

Puzzle 5: **TURNTABLES**

EIGHT turntables are turned.

The sequence is:

N/E/S/W/S/E/N/E

so most of the turns are to tracks taking the engine **EAST**.

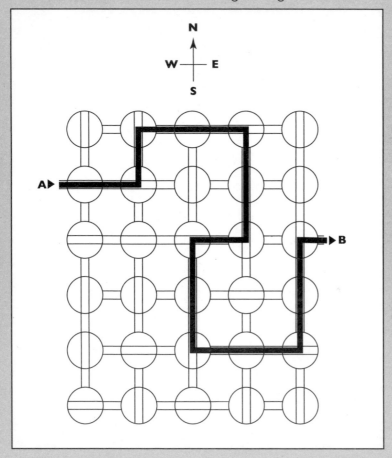

Puzzle 6: **WHO IS IT?**

The mystery personality is **Isambard Kingdom Brunel**.

Puzzle 7: **STATIONGRAM**

The station is **SCARBOROUGH**.

Puzzle 8: **RAILWAY COMPANIES WORD SEARCH**

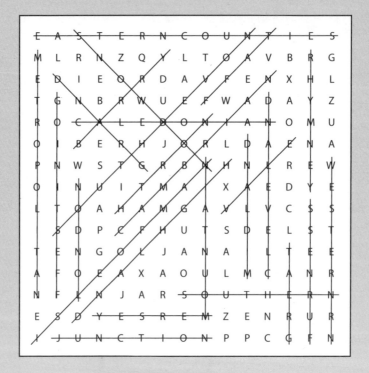

Puzzle 9: **FARE DEAL**

The booking clerk's system was based on the A to Z code, where A = 1, B = 2 etc.

Of the letters in the destinations on page 70 A = 1; B = 2; C = 3; D = 4; E = 5; G = 7; H = 8; I = 9; K = 11; L = 12; N = 14; O = 15; P = 16; R = 18; S = 19; T = 20; W = 23; Y = 25; Z = 26.

The answers are therefore:

BRIGHTON (2 + 18 + 9 + 7 + 8 + 20 + 15 + 14 = 93 which also equals 7s 9d)

GLASGOW (7 + 12 + 1 + 19 + 7 +15 + 23 = 84 which also equals 7s)

LEEDS (12 + 5 + 5 + 4 + 19 = 45 which also equals 3s 9d)

PENZANCE (16 + 5 + 14 + 26 + 1 + 14 + 3 + 5 = 84 which also equals 7s)

YORK (25 + 15 + 18 + 11 = 69 which also equals 5s 9d)

Puzzle 10: **FORWARD SHUNT**

1 Track – Truck; **2** Coach – Couch; **3** Stake – Stoke; **4** Medal – Metal; **5** Steps – Stops.

Puzzle 11: **RECTANGULAR RAIL**

There are **36 rectangles** in the diagram.

The distance of track on the smallest rectangular route is **20 miles**. The biggest rectangle is created by the four outer sides of the plan. This is a square so each side has to be the same length. If four sides **total 80 miles**, then one side will **equal 20 miles**. The smallest rectangle is clearly the one top right of the plan. In fact, it has sides that are exactly a quarter of the length of the outer sides. Therefore the distance around it will be a quarter of the miles in the outer route: **80÷4 = 20**.

Puzzle 12: **SPLITS**

1 Brake/Guard; **2** Speed/Truck; **3** Lines/Train;
4 Bridge/Tunnel; **5** Points/Signal.

Puzzle 13: **A to Z**

The words reading **ACROSS** from left to right, top to bottom are:

Vacant, Stopping, Halt, Local, Exit, First, Journeyed, Bristol, Equipment, Check, Peak, Aisle, Send, Westward, Valley.

The words reading **DOWN** from left to right, top to bottom are:

Magazine, Fastest, Stall, Coal, Speeded, Engine, Crossings, Roof, From, Reconvey, Tickets, Whistle, Queues, Leave, Afar.

1 = B, 2 = R, 3 = I, 4 = S, 5 = T, 6 = O, 7 = L, 8 = J, 9 = A, 10 = V, 11 = H, 12 = F, 13 = Q, 14 = U, 15 = C, 16 = G, 17 = M, 18 = Y, 19 = X, 20 = W, 21 = N, 22 = Z, 23 = P, 24 = K, 25 = D, 26 = E.

The letters that you find from the listed numbers spell out the name of **TEMPLE MEADS** station in Bristol.

Puzzle 14: **FITBACK – ENGINES**

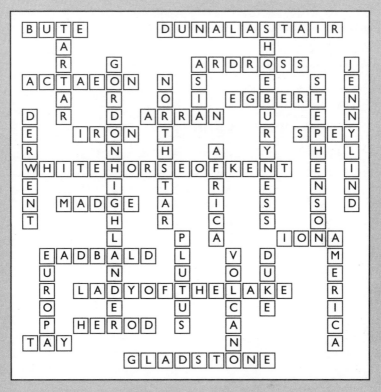

HENGIST is the word that is left over.

Puzzle 15: **CONNECTIONS**

1 Express; **2** Rail; **3** Line; **4** Track; **5** Carriage.

Puzzle 16: **SPECIAL SCOTCH EXPRESS**

When the trains crossed paths, they would both have been at an equal distance from Edinburgh Waverley – and indeed from London Kings Cross.

Puzzle 17: **LOST PROPERTY**

Mr Guard/Raincoat/Waterloo/7 a.m.

Mr Driver/Keys/Paddington/9 a.m.

Mr Porter/Wallet/Euston/6 a.m.

Miss Stokes/Umbrella/Liverpool Street/8 a.m.

Mrs Whistler/Spectacles/Kings Cross/6.30 a.m

Puzzle 18: **MYSTERY OBJECT**

Purpose-built fitted toilet.

Puzzle 19: **FUEL FOR THOUGHT**

1 ton.

Puzzle 20: **GWR**

1 Bristol; **2** Exeter; **3** Maidenhead; **4** Reading; **5** Swindon.

From west to east the locations are Exeter, Bristol, Swindon, Reading and Maidenhead.

Puzzle 21: **GRADIENTS**

The difference between the two journeys is **10 minutes**.

A–E takes **130 minutes** in total:

A–C is 40 miles at 30mph = 80 minutes PLUS C–D is 20 miles at 60mph = 20 minutes PLUS D–E is 20 miles at 40mph = 30 minutes.

E–A takes **120 minutes** in total:

E–D is 20 miles at 30mph = 40 minutes PLUS D–C is 20 miles at 60mph = 20 minutes PLUS C–A is 40 miles at 40mph = 60 minutes.

Puzzle 22: **WHAT AM I?**

STEAM. The first letter is an **S** or a **T**. The second letter is a **T**, and that means the first letter has to be an **S**. The third letter could be a **V**, **E** or **L**. The fourth letter is an **A**. This means that the third letter options of **V** and **L** can be discounted leaving the **E**. The fifth letter could be an **M**, **E** or **S**, but only **M** can be added to the existing letter combination to complete a word.

Puzzle 23: **QUIZ TRAIN**

ACROSS: 3 Derby; **7** George; **8** Opened; **10** Trevithick; **11** Rear; **12** Stall; **13** Sheffield; **16** Eastern; **21** Georgemas; **22** Lochs; **23** Diss; **24** Kings Cross; **26** Renown; **27** Dundee; **28** Gauge.

DOWN: 1 Penrith; **2** Travels; **3** Debt; **4** York; **5** Geordie; **6** Derails; **9** Night Trains; **14** Fare; **15** Race; **17** Devizes; **18** Bristol; **19** Touring; **20** Chester; **24** King; **25** Side.

Puzzle 24: **FOURTH BRIDGE**

Puzzle 25: **STATIONGRAM**

The station is **LLANDUDNO**.

Puzzle 26: **MEMORY TEST**

1 The London, Midland and Scottish Railway; **2** *Rocket*; **3** Princess (Royal); **4** Right; **5** Progress; **6** 1830; **7** Two; **8** Old locomotives; **9** Two; **10** Red.

SECTION THREE

Puzzle 1: **MURDER ON THE MIDNIGHT EXPRESS**

The murderer was Claude Battersby-Smythe, Lord Crusty's cousin, who was seen with the flowers in the restaurant car.

The other guests were located as follows:

Lord Tony Broke/Biographer/Briefcase/Sleeper.

Myrtle Overbrightly/Personal Assistant/Typewriter/1st-class compartment.

Olga/Solicitor/Cane/Corridor.

Professor Wilde/Ex-colleague/Tray/2nd-class compartment.

Puzzle 2: **STATIONGRAM**

The station is **INVERNESS**.

Puzzle 3: **FAMOUS NUMBER**

The number is **4468**, which is the number of the famous Class A4 locomotive that set steam speed records, *Mallard*.

6 x 8 = 48. Reading the first digit and final digit together gives 48.

Puzzle 4: **A to Z**

The words reading **ACROSS** from left to right, top to bottom are:

Way out; Standard; Iron; Ridge; Link; Carry; Overnight; Express; Cafeteria; Turns; Sits; Pence; Late; Charging; Motion.

The words reading **DOWN** from left to right, top to bottom are:

Carriage; Country; Start; Gaze; Idyllic; Branch; Diversion; Rest; Axle; Junction; Leisure; Quality; Alight; Terms; Paid.

1 = E, 2 = X, 3 = P, 4 = R, 5 = S, 6 = O, 7 = L, 8 = B, 9 = F, 10 = N, 11 = Z, 12 = Y, 13 = A, 14 = H, 15 = G, 16 = Q, 17 = M, 18 = C, 19 = I, 20 = J, 21 = V, 22 = T, 23 = D, 24 = U, 25 = K, 26 = W.

The letters that you find from these numbers spell out the name of a famous **EXPRESS** train called **CORONATION SCOT**.

Puzzle 5: **A PENNY A MILE**

The return journey was **24 miles**, 12 miles each way.

The cheaper tickets would have cost a shilling each way as there were 12 pennies in a shilling. The first-class ticket would have cost 1 shilling and sixpence (half as much again).

The journey would have cost 4 shillings and sixpence each way, making 9 shillings in all, so Mr Tripp would have had a shilling change from his 10 shilling note.

Puzzle 6: **CLOCKWORK**

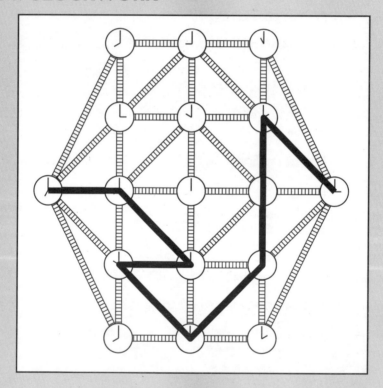

Puzzle 7: **WHAT AM I?**

VIADUCT. There are no options for the first three letters. The fourth letter is a **D** or an **O**. As the first three letters are **V**, **I**, **A**, the **O** can be discounted leaving the **D**. There are no options for the fifth, sixth and seventh letters.

Puzzle 8: **CONNECTIONS**

1 Yard; **2** Bridge; **3** Book; **4** Signal; **5** Ticket.

Puzzle 9: **QUOTA**

1 Carriage; **2** Holidays; **3** Evacuees; **4** *Scotsman*; **5** Trolleys; **6** Electric; **7** Rush Hour; **8** Tourists; **9** Off / Book; **10** Networks.

The author was **(G.K.) CHESTERTON,** who said the only way of catching a train he ever discovered was '**TO MISS THE TRAIN BEFORE**'.

Puzzle 10: **SINGLE TRACK**

Down train: Part; Ram; Said; Nine; Power; Bleep.

Up train: Peel; Brew; Open; India; Smart; Rap.

The operation to evacuate children at the outbreak of the Second World War was called **PIED PIPER**.

Puzzle 11: **CIRCULAR TOUR**

Charles got on at Northfields and off at Southfields.

Valerie got on at Eastfields and off at Northfields.

Peter got on at Southfields and off at Westfields.

Elizabeth got on at Westfields and off at Eastfields.

Puzzle 12: **STATIONGRAM**

The station is **BARNSTAPLE**.

Puzzle 13: **RESTRICTIONS**

The average speed is **40 miles per hour**. The train spends 5 minutes covering 5 miles before the restricted area, and spends a further 5 minutes covering another 5 miles after leaving the zone. The train when travelling at 30 miles per hour will spend 20 minutes covering 10 miles. That makes a total of 30 minutes to cover 20 miles. That gives an average of 40 miles per hour.

Puzzle 14: **ALL CHANGE**

ACROSS: 7 Rate; **9** Direct; **10** Reverse; **11** Named; **12** Ends; **13** Rails; **17** Route; **18** Line; **22** Raced; **23** Notices; **24** Inland; **25** Fare.

DOWN: 1 Boarded; **2** Provide; **3** Start; **4** Signals; **5** Teams; **6** Study; **9** Departing; **14** Loading; **15** Circles; **16** Seaside; **19** Train; **20** Scale; **21** Steam.

Puzzle 15: **FULL SPEED AHEAD**

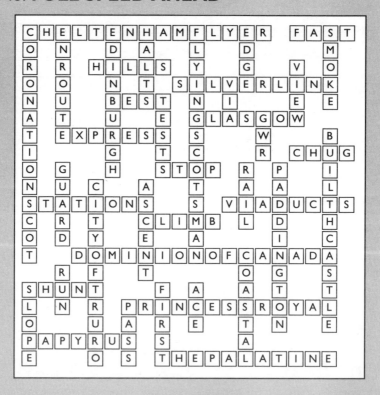

LONDON is the word that doesn't fit in the grid.

Puzzle 16: **SPLITS**

1 Coach/Meals; **2** Driver/Siding; **3** Buffet/Engine; **4** Diesel/Porter; **5** Return/Single.

Puzzle 17: **WHO IS IT?**

The fictional mystery personality is Agatha Christie's heroine **Miss Marple**. The novel was the *4.50 From Paddington*.

Puzzle 18: **SEASIDE SHUFFLE**

1 Brighton; **2** Morecambe; **3** Penzance; **4** Skegness; **5** Southend.

The most northerly location is Morecambe. Move south and east to Skegness. Move south and east to Southend. South and west is Brighton. Penzance is the most westerly of the stations.

Puzzle 19: **BRIEF ENCOUNTER**

Puzzle 20: **MILEAGE MATCH**

1 = d), **2** = a), **3** = c), **4** = e), **5** = b)

Puzzle 21: **WHAT'S THE LINK?**

1 Black; **2** Red; **3** White.

The link is **COLOUR**. These colours complete the station names.

Puzzle 22: **STATIONGRAM**

The station is **HARROGATE**.

Puzzle 23: **MYSTERY OBJECT**

The mystery object is **Mallard**.

Puzzle 24: **QUIZ TRAIN**

ACROSS: **3** Dover; **7** Gretna; **8** Exeter; **10** Maidenhead; **11** Eton; **12** Set up; **13** Stopovers; **16** Colours; **21** Eastbound; **22** Cheap; **23** Edge; **24** *Coronation*; **26** Effect; **27** Silver; **28** Yards.

DOWN: **1** Greased; **2** Stadium; **3** Dawn; **4** Read; **5** Reserve; **6** Detours; **9** West Country; **14** Port; **15** Soho; **17** Cardiff; **18** Steered; **19** Shuttle; **20** May Owen; **24** *City*; **25** Ness.

Puzzle 25: **BOOKSTALL**

The author was **Edith Nesbit** and the book was *The Railway Children*.

Puzzle 26: **MEMORY TEST**

1 King's Cross; **2** Pullman; **3** Three hours; **4** Two; **5** Gentleman; **6** Leeds and Ripon; **7** Restaurant/dining car; **8** Red; **9** Hills; **10** Newcastle.

Puzzle 1: **TRAINSPOTTING**

6	9	2	5	1	7	4	8	3
5	3	1	8	6	4	9	7	2
8	7	4	2	3	9	5	1	6
4	1	9	6	7	3	2	5	8
7	5	3	9	2	8	6	4	1
2	6	8	1	4	5	3	9	7
3	4	6	7	9	1	8	2	5
9	8	7	3	5	2	1	6	4
1	2	5	4	8	6	7	3	9

The shaded squares reveal the number **4472**. This was the number given to the world-famous *Flying Scotsman* after it appeared at the Empire Exhibition in Wembley in 1924.

Puzzle 2: **DRONE RANGER**

The drone had travelled **35 miles**.

The trains will meet halfway between their destinations. As the journey is 60 miles in total, they must have both travelled 30 miles. The drone is moving at 70 miles an hour, and in 30 minutes will have travelled 35 miles.

Puzzle 3: **THE BEECHING AXE**

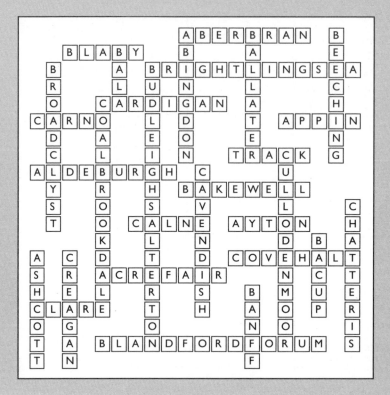

Puzzle 4: **RAILWAYANIA**

Valued at £1,000 the enamel sign was previously bought at an auction.

Valued at £500 the station clock came from a charity sale.

Valued at £100 the poster had been given as a gift.

Valued at £50 the lamp had been found stored away in a loft.

Valued at £20 the box of timetables had been handed down through the family.

Puzzle 5: **STATIONGRAM**

The station is **GLASGOW CENTRAL**.

Puzzle 6: **A to Z**

The words reading **ACROSS** from left to right, top to bottom are:

Camera; Souvenir; Zone; Noisy; Edge; Class; High Speed; Fireman; Guard's van; Board; Shop; Style; Pass; Altitude; One way.

The words reading **DOWN** from left to right, top to bottom are:

Wagon lit; Reverse; Jaunt; Quay; Receipt; Single; Itinerary; Heat; Kids; Eurostar; Prepaid Complex; Uphill; Depot; Shut.

1 = C, 2 = L, 3 = A, 4 = S, 5 = N, 6 = P, 7 = Q, 8 = H, 9 = Y, 10 = B, 11 = O, 12 = R, 13 = T, 14 = F, 15 = W, 16 = J, 17 = Z, 18 = U, 19 = I, 20 = D, 21 = M, 22 = E, 23 = V, 24 = G, 25 = X, 26 = K.

The letters that you find from the listed numbers spell out the name of Prime Minister **HAROLD MACMILLAN**. [4]

Puzzle 7: **HIDDEN FINDS**

1 WiFi; **2** Plug; **3** App; **4** Screen; **5** Laptop.

Puzzle 8: **BOOKSTALL**

The author was **J. K. Rowling** and the book was *Harry Potter and the Philosopher's Stone.*

Puzzle 9: **ENGINE RESTORATION**

Andrew/shed B/16 hours/4-6-2

Graham/shed C/10 hours/2-2-2

Joe/shed E/14 hours/2-8-2

Ken/shed D/8 hours/0-6-2

Mike/shed A/20 hours/4-4-0

Puzzle 10: **HERITAGE**

1 Bluebell; **2** Dartmoor; **3** Midland; **4** Caledonian; **5** Llangollen.

The most westerly Heritage Railway is the Dartmoor Railway. Move east to the Bluebell Railway in East Sussex. From there go north first to the Midland Railway near Nottingham and then to the Caledonian Railway in the east of Scotland. Finally go back south to the Llangollen Railway in North Wales.

Puzzle 11: **KEEPING TRACK**

Trains depart from **PLATFORM 3** to arrive at New Street station, with **FIVE** stations along the route.

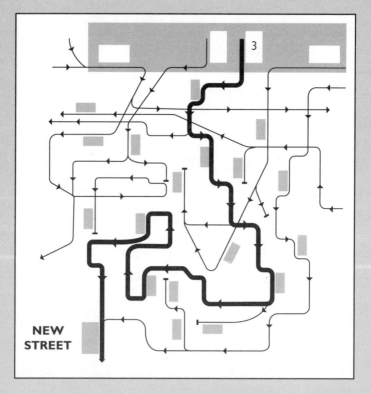

Puzzle 12: **SPLITS**

1 Fares/Shunt; **2** Depot/Goods; **3** Change/Ticket; **4** Barrier/Station; **5** Freight/Service.

Puzzle 13: **QUOTA**

1 Waterloo; **2** Initials; **3** Lunches; **4** Luggage; **5** Intercom; **6** App / Hall; **7** Main line; **8** Advanced; **9** Warnings; **10** Download; **11** Railcard; **12** York / Map

The author is **WILLIAM AWDRY**, the Rev Awdry who wrote the *Thomas the Tank Engine* books.

He is quoted as saying, '**A STEAM ENGINE HAS ALWAYS GOT CHARACTER**.' He adds, 'It's the most human of all man-made machines.'

Puzzle 14: **MYSTERY OBJECT**

The mystery object is **Bradshaw's Railway Guide**.

Puzzle 15: **STATIONGRAM**

The station is **NOTTINGHAM**.

Puzzle 16: **WHO IS IT?**

The mystery personality is **Michael Portillo**.

Puzzle 17: **WHAT AM I?**

The answer is **BRIDGE**. There are no options for the first, second, third, fourth and sixth letters. The fifth could be a **G** or **U**, but only **G** will make a word.

Puzzle 18: **SINGLE TRACK**

Down train: Taps; Too; Beer; Gala; Vowel; Broom.

Up train: Moor; Blew; Oval; Agree; Boots; Pat.

The famous station terminus is **WATERLOO** (it was the London Eurostar terminus from 1994 to 2007).

Puzzle 19: **POINTS**

The word is **CAR**. It makes the words **CARTON**, **CARPET** and **CARROT**.

Puzzle 20: **A CLASS ACT**

The answer is **Class 29**.

Written in capitals as **TWENTYNINE**, it contains that number of straight lines.

The class comprised 20 diesel-electric Bo-Bo locomotives used for both passenger and freight services.

Puzzle 21: **CHANNEL TUNNEL**

FOLKESTONE appears twice.

Puzzle 22: **QUIZ TRAIN**

ACROSS: 3 Cocoa; **7** Boiler; **8** Pick up; **10** Crosswords; **11** Enid; **12** Ascot; **13** St Pancras; **16** Classes; **21** Transport; **22** Guard; **23** Hall; **24** Mail trains; **26** Lounge; **27** Booked; **28** Table.

DOWN: 1 Tourist; **2** Glasgow; **3** Crew; **4** Apps; **5** Science; **6** Musical; **9** British Rail; **14** Axed; **15** Slip; **17** Creator; **18** England; **19** Curator; **20** Branded; **24** Meet; **25** Tube.

Puzzle 23: **STATIONGRAM**

The station is **EDINBURGH WAVERLEY**.

Puzzle 24: **HOME RUN**

Mrs Brown, a social worker, read a magazine and got out at the sixth station.

Mrs Patel, a secretary, read her laptop and got out at the seventh station.

Mr Khan, a lawyer, read a paperback novel and got out at the eighth station.

Mr Wilson, a librarian, read a newspaper and got out at the ninth station.

Mr James, an accountant, read text messages on his smart phone and got out at the tenth – and last – stop.

Puzzle 25: **CONNECTIONS**

1 Stock; **2** Tunnel; **3** Table; **4** Fare; **5** Service.

Puzzle 26: **MEMORY TEST**

1 Four; **2** West; **3** Swansea; **4** Cardiff; **5** Pocket timetable; **6** Gain and Train; **7** 125; **8** Red; **9** Bath; **10** Easy.

ENDNOTES

SECTION ONE

[1] S. Hughes, *Copperopolis: Landscapes of the Early Industrial Period in Swansea* (Cardiff: Royal Commission on the Ancient and Historical Monuments of Wales, 2008), 157; R. Jenkins, 'The Society for the Mines Royal and the German Colony in the Lake District', *Transactions of the Newcomen Society,* 18 (1938), 226–227.

[2] M. J. T. Lewis, *Early Wooden Railways* (London: Routledge Kegan Paul, 1974), 1–3.

[3] Lewis, *Early Wooden Railways,* 92–93.

[4] J. Simmons, *The Railways of Britain* (London: Macmillan, 1986), 10.

[5] O. S. Nock, *Locomotion: A World Survey of Railway Traction* (London: Routledge & Kegan Paul, 1975), 9.

[6] L. T. C. Rolt, *The Railway Revolution: George and Robert Stephenson* (London: Longman, 1960), 50.

[7] See: W. T. Jackman, *The Development of Transportation in Modern England, Vol. 2* (Cambridge: Cambridge University Press, 1916), 507–509; M. Macnair, *William James (1771–1837): The Man Who Discovered George Stephenson* (King's Lynn: Railway & Canal Historical Society, 2007).

[8] M. W. Kirby, *The Origins of Railway Enterprise: The Stockton & Darlington Railway, 1821–1863* (Cambridge: Cambridge University Press, 2002), 30.

[9] T. R. Pearce, *The Locomotives of the Stockton & Darlington Railway* (Southwell: The Historical Model Railway Society, 1996), 1.

[10] T. R. Gourvish, 'Railways 1830–70: The Formative Years' in *Transport in Victorian Britain,* ed. M. J. Freeman and D. H. Aldcroft (Manchester: Manchester University Press), 57.

[11] The disadvantages of canal transport were emphasised in a letter published by Joseph Sandars the year the first bill was thrown out of Parliament. See: J. Sandars, *A Letter on the Subject of the Projected Rail Road between Liverpool and Manchester (4th Edition)* (Liverpool: W. Wales & Co., 1825), 22–23.

[12] 'Opening of the Manchester and Liverpool Railway', *Derby Mercury*, 15 Sep. 1830, 2.

[13] 'Opening of the Liverpool & Manchester Railway', *Morning Post*, 18 Sep. 1830, 2.

[14] J. S. Walker, *An Accurate Description of the Liverpool & Manchester Railway and the Branch Railways (with an Account of the Opening of the Railway), 3rd Edition* (Liverpool: J. F. Cannell, 1832), 45; 'Opening of the Manchester and Liverpool Railway', *Hereford Journal*, 22 Sep. 1830, 2.

SECTION TWO

[1] H. J. Dyos and D. H. Aldcroft, *British Transport: An Economic Survey from the Seventeenth Century to the Twentieth* (Leicester: Leicester University Press, 1969), 123.

[2] Dyos and Aldcroft, *British Transport*, 118–119.

[3] R. Leleux, *A Regional History of the Railways of Great Britain, Vol. 9: East Midlands* (Newton Abbot: David & Charles, 1984), 110.

[4] E. T. MacDermot (revised by C. R. Clinker), *History of the Great Western Railway: Vol. 1, 1833–1863* (London: Ian Allan, 1972), 3, 16.

[5] I. K. Brunel, *Minutes of Evidence*, Great Western Bill, 24 July 1835; D. Hodgkins, 'The GWR Comes to London – Why Paddington?', *Railway & Canal Historical Society Journal*, 36:7 (2010), 44–45.

[6] J. Simmons, *The Railways of Britain* (London: Macmillan, 1986), 26.

[7] M. Casson, *The World's First Railway System: Enterprise, Competition and Regulation on the Railway Network in Victorian Britain* (Oxford: Oxford University Press, 2009), 17; T. R. Gourvish, *Railways and the British Economy, 1830–1914* (London: Macmillan, 1980), 12.

[8] R. Beaumont, *The Railway King: A Biography of George Hudson* (London: Review, 2002), 65–66; G. Channon, *Railways in Britain and the United States, 1830–1940: Studies in Economic and Business History* (Aldershot: Ashgate, 2001), 37.

[9] Casson, *The World's First Railway System*, 44; K. G. Fenelon, Railway Economics (London: Methuen & Co., 1991), 8.

[10] J. Winton, *The Little Wonder: The Story of the Ffestiniog Railway* (London: Michael Joseph, 1975), 16.

[11] 'Virtual Dethronement of the Railway King', *Bradford Observer*, 8 Mar. 1849, 6; Rolt, *The Railway Revolution*, 271.

[12] A. W. Skempton, 'Embankments and Cuttings on the Early Railways', *Construction History*, 11 (1996), 39.

[13] D. Brooke, 'The Railway Navvy: A Reassessment', *Construction History*, 5 (1989), 39.

[14] Brooke, 'The Railway Navvy: A Reassessment', 38–39.

[15] T. Coleman, *The Railway Navvies: A History of the Men Who Made the Railways* (London: Pimlico, 2000), 123; G. Dow, *Great Central, Vol. 1: The Progenitors, 1813–1863* (London: Locomotive Publishing Company, 1959), 64.

[16] S. Bradley, *The Railways: Nation, Network, People* (London: Profile Books, 2015), 88–100; S. Major, *Early Victorian Railway Excursions: 'The Million Go Forth'* (Barnsley: Pen & Sword, 2015), 17–18, 24.

[17] C. J. Allen, *The Great Eastern Railway (Fourth Ed.)* (London: Ian Allan, 1967), 63.

[18] S. T. Abernethy, 'Opening up the Suburbs: Workmen's Trains in London, 1816–1914', *Urban History*, 42:1 (2014), 79; C. Heap and J. van Riemsdijk, *The Pre-grouping Railways, part two* (London: HMSO, 1980), 21.

[19] H. Pollins, *Britain's Railways: An Industrial History* (Newton Abbot: David & Charles, 1971), 63.

[20] Simmons, *The Railways of Britain*, 195.

[21] Skempton, 'Embankments and Cuttings on the Early Railways', 43.

[22] Railway Regulation Act, 1844, 7 & 8 Vict., 85.

[23] G. Kitchenside, *150 Years of Railway Carriages* (Newton Abbot: David & Charles, 1981), 16.

[24] Kitchenside, *150 Years of Railway Carriages*, 16.

[25] L. T. C. Rolt, *Red for Danger (New edition)* (Stroud: Sutton, 2007), 19; Bradley, *The Railways*, 60–61.

[26] Rolt, *Red for Danger*, 152.

SECTION THREE

[1] S. Ward, *Selling Places: The Marketing and Promotion of Towns and Cities, 1850–2000* (London: E. & F. N. Spon, 1998), 95.

[2] J. Armstrong and T. Gourvish, 'London's Railways – Their Contribution to Solving the Problem of Growth and Expansion', *Japan Railway and Transport Review*, 23 (2000), 5.

[3] M. C. Duffy, *Electric Railways, 1880–1990* (London: Institution of Engineering and Technology, 2008), 79, 83; D. Brown, *Southern Electric: A New History, Vol. 1* (London: Capital Transport, 2010), 11.

[4] 'The New Motor Car Service', *Great Western Railway Magazine*, XV (1903), 117; C. R. Clinker, *Great Western Railway: A Register of Halts and Platforms, 1903–1975* (C. R. Clinker: Padstow, 1975), 1.

5 A. Chadwick et al., *The Meat Trade Vol. I* (London: Gresham Publishing Co., 1935), 139; J. B. Jefferys, *Retail Trading in Britain, 1850–1950* (Cambridge: Cambridge University Press, 1954), 182.

6 For example, see: 'Collecting Five Million Gallons of Milk a Year', *The Commercial Motor*, XLVII (August 7, 1928), 844–847.

7 J. A. B. Hamilton, *Britain's Railways in World War I* (London: George Allen & Unwin, 1967), 38–39.

8 A. Lambert, *Britain's Railways in Wartime* (Swindon: Historic England, 2018), 66; Hamilton, *Britain's Railways in World War I*, 30.

9 H. Wojtczak, *Railwaywomen: Exploitation, Betrayal and Triumph in the Workplace* (Hastings: Hastings Press, 2003), 43–114; Lambert, *Britain's Railways in Wartime*, 66; Hamilton, *Britain's Railways in World War I*, 174–175.

10 T. Gibson, *Road Haulage by Motor in Britain: The First Forty Years* (Aldershot: Ashgate, 2001), 45.

11 Gibson, *Road Haulage by Motor in Britain*, 119.

12 P. Scott, 'British Railways and the Challenge from Road Haulage, 1919–1939', *Twentieth Century British History*, 13 (2002), 103; Gibson, *Road Haulage by Motor in Britain*, 138.

13 M. R. Bonavia, *The Four Great Railways* (Newton Abbot: David & Charles, 1980), 176; D. L. Munby, *Inland Transport Statistics: Great Britain, 1900–1970, Vol. I* (Oxford: Clarendon Press, 1978), Table A10.

14 Bonavia, *The Four Great Railways*, 181.

15 Railway Companies Association, *Fair Play for the Railways* (1932), 5, 13–14; O. H. Mance, *The Road and Rail Transport Problem* (London: Pitman, 1941), 112; P. Bagwell, *The Transport Revolution (2nd Edition)* (London: Routledge, 1988), 246.

16 Lambert, *Britain's Railways in Wartime*, 141.

[17] A. J. Mullay, *For the King's Service: Railway Ships at War* (Easingwold: Pendragon Publishing, 2008), 79.

[18] P. Tatlow, *Return from Dunkirk, Railways to the Rescue: Operation Dynamo (1940)* (Usk: Oakwood Press, 2010), 85.

[19] B. W. L. Brooksbank, *London Mainline War Damage* (London: Capital Transport, 2007), 88–92.

[20] M. D. Rowland, 'London's Milk Supplies in Wartime', *Our Notebook*, 20 (Spring 1941), 5.

[21] Rowland, 'London's Milk Supplies in Wartime', 6.

[22] R. Bell, *History of the British Railways during the War, 1939–45* (London: The Railway Gazette, 1946), 144.

[23] R. Milward, 'Industrial Organisation and Economic Factors in Nationalisation' in *The Political Economy of Nationalisation in Britain, 1920–1950*, ed. R. Millward and J. Singleton (Cambridge: Cambridge University Press, 1995), 5.

[24] R. Hendry, *The Changing Face of Britain's Railways, 1938–1953: The Railway Companies Bow Out* (Stamford: Dalrymple & Verdun, 2005), 28–30; T. R. Gourvish, *British Railways, 1948–73* (Cambridge: Cambridge University Press, 1986), 6; M. R. Bonavia, *The Organisation of British Railways* (London: Ian Allan, 1971), 34–35; 'Victory and After', *London & North Eastern Railway Magazine*, 35 (1945), 102.

[25] G. Crompton, 'The Railway Companies, 1920–1950' in *The Political Economy of Nationalisation in Britain, 1920–1950*, ed. R. Millward and J. Singleton (Cambridge: Cambridge University Press, 1995), 140; HC Deb 17 December 1946, vol 431, col 1809.

[26] Hendry, *The Changing Face of Britain's Railways*, 31–32.

[27] Hendry, *The Changing Face of Britain's Railways*, 64.

SECTION FOUR

[1] T. R. Gourvish, *British Railways, 1948–73* (Cambridge: Cambridge University Press, 1986), 55.

[2] Quoted in *Gourvish, British Railways, 1948–73*, 258.

[3] 'Capital Spending on Railways', *Financial Times*, 25 Oct. 1954, 6.

[4] Gourvish, *British Railways, 1948–73*, 259.

[5] D. H. Aldcroft, *British Railways in Transition: The Economic Problems of Britain's Railways since 1914* (London: Macmillan, 1968), 158.

[6] Gourvish, *British Railways, 1948–73*, 270.

[7] D. N. Clough, *The Modernisation Plan: British Railways' Blueprint for the Future* (Hersham: Ian Allan, 2014), 76–78, 127–128.

[8] Aldcroft, *British Railways in Transition*, 158.

[9] R. H. N. Hardy, *Beeching: Champion of the Railway?* (London: Ian Allan, 1989), 46.

[10] British Railways, *The Reshaping of the Railways Part I: Report* (London: HMSO, 1963), 10; Gourvish, *British Railways, 1948–73*, 403.

[11] Aldcroft, *British Railways in Transition*, 184. See also G. Findlay, *The Working and Management of an English Railway*, 3rd Edition (London: Whittaker & Co., 1890), 266–267.

[12] Gourvish, *British Railways, 1948–73*, 490–491; Aldcroft, *British Railways in Transition*, 204; British Railways Board, *The Development of the Major Railway Trunk Routes* (London: British Railways Board, 1965), 30.

[13] P. Brabham, *Barry: The History of the Yard and its Locomotives* (Hersham: Oxford Publishing Company, 2013), 52–53.

[14] R. Arnott, *TOPS: The Story of a British Railways Project* (London: British Railways Board, 1979), 1.

[15] Department of Transport, *Railway Finances: Report of a Committee Chaired by Sir David Serpell KCB CMG OBE* (London: HMSO, 1983), 7–8.

[16] Department of Transport, *Railway Finances*, 68–69.

[17] P. Thalmann, *The Dynamics of Freight Transport Development* (Aldershot: Ashgate, 2004), 27.

[18] N. Faith, *The History of the Channel Tunnel* (Barnsley: Pen & Sword, 2018), 90–121.

[19] S. Glaister, 'British Rail Privatisation – Competition Destroyed by Politics', *University of Bath: Centre for the Study of Regulated Industries Occasional Paper No. 23* (November 2004), 7.

[20] Glaister, 'British Rail Privatisation', 8, 33–35.

[21] Glaister, 'British Rail Privatisation', 37–40.

IMAGE CREDITS

RAILWAY MUSEUM

First opened in 1975 in York, the National Railway Museum is home to many world-famous locomotives and an unrivalled collection that celebrates the past, present and future of innovation on the railways. Dedicated to igniting visitors' curiosity about the people, places and engineering marvels behind the railways, the museum's staff and volunteers put their passion for amazing stories into everything they do.